RADICAL PROBLEMS, SIMPLE SOLUTIONS

How Markets can Help Fix the Retirement Crisis and Solve Wealth Inequality

ISBN 979-8-218-20437-2

Library of Congress Control Number: 2023910007

Cover Design by Strategy Studios

RADICAL PROBLEMS, SIMPLE SOLUTIONS

How Markets can Help Fix the Retirement Crisis and Solve Wealth Inequality

MIKE MACMILLAN

“

Some real common sense, from a common sense kind of dude, rife with cultural references and inspiration chronicling the modern digital narrative. Insightful and fun to read too.

—Andy Serwer, Editor at Large at Barron’s, former Editor in Chief Yahoo Finance, former Editor of Fortune

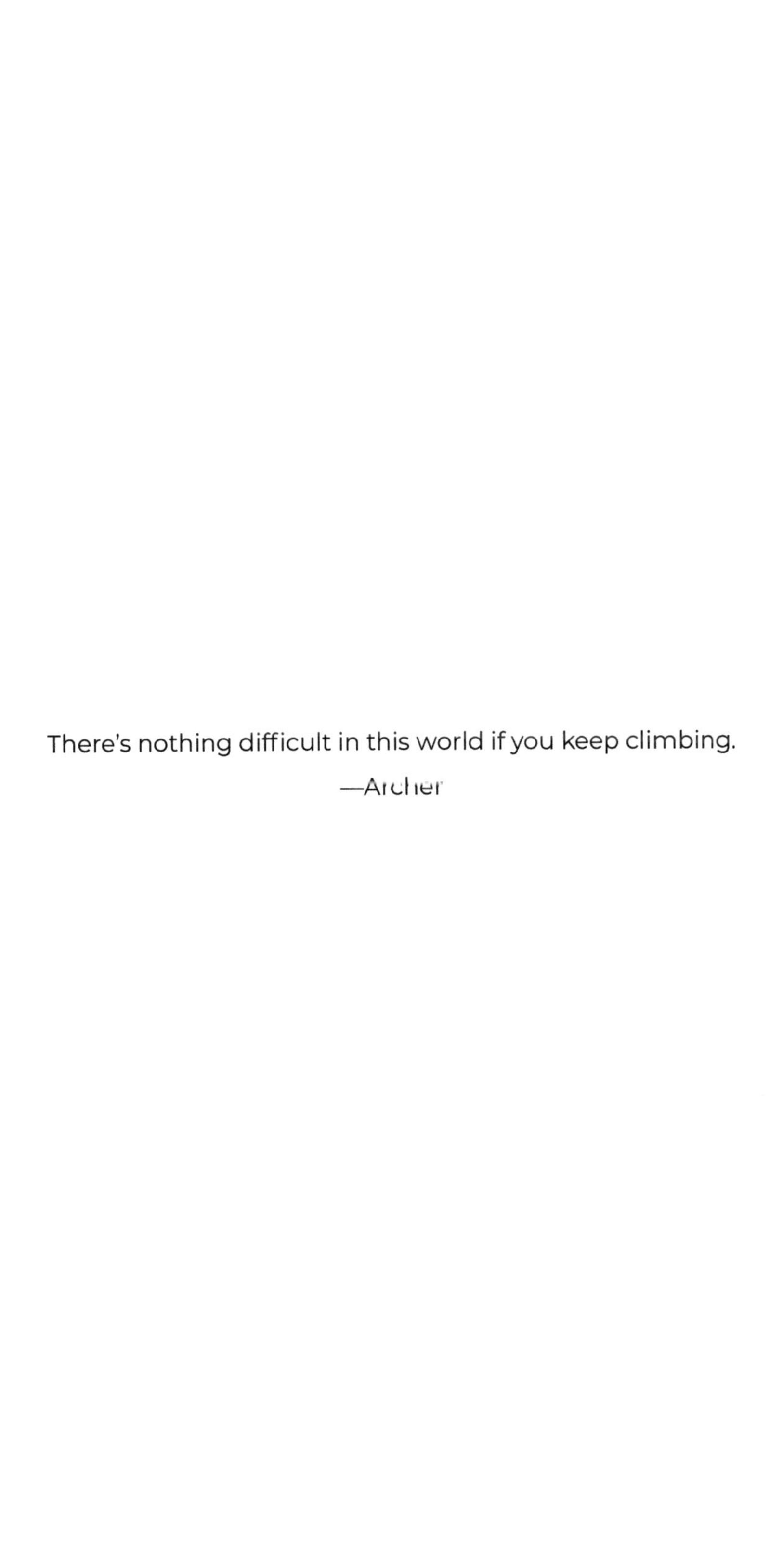

There's nothing difficult in this world if you keep climbing.

—Archer

Table of Contents

It's a Wreck.

Introduction

Everything goes south

THE FIRST FEW WEEKS WERE eye-opening. It was mind-bogglingly quiet, especially for someone used to commuting to New York. It was dark at night, really dark. There were noises out there in the woods.

After a week or two of that I started to think about self-defense. As a result, I now have my first gun permit. Cost: $5. Downside: it's one permit per handgun (no permit required for shotguns), so if you want to build an arsenal it's going to cost you. Amusing aside: when I went to pick up the form at the courthouse and plucked down my five bucks, the woman there asked me, "Just one, honey?"

I felt a little sheepish to admit that, yes, just one. Worst yet, my brother had recommended a six-shot revolver when I had my eye on a 9mm Glock with a 12-shot clip. "Don't want to make this too complicated," he said.

Indeed. Things were complicated enough. Perhaps I was a little hasty, in selling my business in New York City, in convincing my wife that we should explore a new life in North Carolina, in the whole idea of "retiring." A recent piece in *The Wall Street Journal* explained why King Lear is Shakespeare's greatest play. Mainly, I gathered, because Lear was a fool. That makes him human, more or less like the rest of us. Lear had three daughters. I have three daughters. Enough said.

At any rate, the other night there was a rattling of gun fire from a trailer park a half mile away through the woods. I tried to convince myself it was fireworks. I wondered how many gun permits they had.

So this is the country – part Green Acres, part Wes Anderson film. Maybe the truth is that nothing can really prepare you for something so life changing. That realization is, in brief, how this book came to be: an effort to come to terms with the aftermath of the headlong collision of dreams and reality. But what began as a disquisition on the perils of retirement and purposelessness (and, let's be honest, one with a high likelihood of turning unreadably maudlin) slowly morphed into something more hardheaded. It began to shift to addressing the retirement crisis writ large, and to identifying solutions informed by my three decades of experience in the financial services public relations industry in New York City. It would focus not so much on the personal or on the political, but on the practical.

Because as it turns out, it's nice to have a dream but it's better to have a dream and a few dollars set aside. This is an issue that can't be magically addressed at the moment of retirement. You can sit in the dark and yell at the past but you can't change it, as the unnamed protagonist in Delmore Schwartz's 1934 short story, "In Dreams Begin Responsibilities," discovers. Past and present are engaged in ways that aren't always easy to discern, a kind of quantum entanglement. But you can draw a straight line from the money you didn't save and invest in your twenties to the money you don't have now. That's just geometry.

Not saving and not investing has been a way of life for generations of Americans, even as the country's overall wealth has grown. Somewhere around 60%, or 166 million people, live paycheck to paycheck, including eight million who make more than $100,000 a year, and the number has been rising. This doesn't have to be. Even for those with modest incomes there are opportunities to create wealth. Technology has evolved to make this possible in a way it wasn't before, lowering costs and increasing accessibility. The issue now is more about education and awareness, and less about money.

Wall Street has historically cultivated a druidic-like mystery around the markets, but that, too, has started to fall away in an era of no-cost trades, fractional shares, social media, and meme stocks. Early on, the media paid little attention to the asset management business on the theory that there wasn't much of an audience for it. A Wall Street Journal reporter once told me with regards to hedge funds, "We cover three types of stories: the guy who makes a billion, the guy who loses a billion, and the guy who steals a billion."

These days financial news is everywhere from Reddit to TikTok influencers. Not all of this is good – it's safe to say that for the average investor, a lot of it is *not* good – but it has undeniably raised awareness.

Wealth inequality is corrosive but eating the rich isn't really the answer. Here and elsewhere all manner of redistribution schemes have been tried. Those that work tend to cripple economic growth; those that don't, well why bother? There was a story that made the rounds during the 1980s. Deng Xiaoping, the chairman of the Chinese Communist party and the individual most credited with setting that country on the road to freer markets, is having dinner with Lee Kuan Yew, the prime minister of Singapore, a nation state with around five million people. Lee is lecturing Deng on how to run a country. Deng, who oversees a population of more than one billion, listens politely for a time and then says, "Thank you for your advice. That will come in handy if I ever become mayor of Shanghai."

Something similar holds for the U.S. We can't be Finland (apparently the happiest country in the world), and we are definitely not Singapore. We are too big, too complicated, too unruly. We have to find our own way to address the crisis of wealth inequality, one aligned with our historical values: self-reliance and the willingness to sacrifice in one generation to improve the prospects of the next.

In the chapters that follow, I hope to provide some insight into how changes in the world of finance are making this possible.

Everybody's a Winner.

CHAPTER ONE

The Four Stages of Retirement Grief

AS I DISCOVERED, THERE ARE the four stages of retirement grief: shock, denial, hysterical crying, and playing the lottery. North Carolina was a late comer to the lottery – the Reverend Billy Graham was not a fan – but it's making up for lost time. Two-dollar tickets, hundred million dollar pots, and 300 million to one odds. In my younger days I liked to cite Ben Johnson's remark on gambling as a "tax on fools" but from close up you could see why people played. In a life without a lot of hope two dollars buys the chance to dream.

There's a gas station and convenience store few miles from our house. It serves sandwiches and hot food and it's popular with guys in pickup trucks pulling trailers carrying zero-turn mowers. A hard working crowd, mostly Hispanic. On one occasion, I watched as a punter went back to his car to search for change under the seats so he could buy a ticket. This was for the North Carolina "Education Lottery." Clearly a lot of people were getting schooled.

Typical of these state-sponsored numbers games, by the way, there is no dedicated allocation of lottery proceeds to teacher pay or to education in general. The hundreds of millions of dollars lifted from mostly working class pockets goes into the state's general fund. These monies are, as North Carolina's attorney general has said, "fungible."

At any rate, as a retirement strategy playing the lottery leaves something to be desired. Stocks are generally a better bet. But the stock market and the lottery do have one thing in common – you have to be in it to win it. With the lottery, the earlier you start the bigger your lifetime losses, but with the stock market, it's just the opposite. The five, ten, twenty dollars a week thrown at Pick Six or Mega Millions would, if invested in an S&P 500 index fund and left there for 40 years, return real money.

Of course it doesn't move in a straight line. In my lifetime, I've seen five major market crashes: in 1987, when stocks fell 25% in a day, the Asian Debt Crisis in 1997, the Dot Com Crash in 2001, the Real Estate debacle in 2007-2008, and the coronavirus crash, also known as the Great Cessation. You kind of expect to lose when you play the lottery; most people aren't really prepared to lose half the value of their portfolio in a week. But it happens.

There's a difference, though. Markets bounce back.

That's entertainment.

CHAPTER TWO

Meanwhile, back in New York

FOR MORE THAN 30 YEARS I worked in financial services public relations in New York City. We represented mutual fund managers and investment banks, financial technology companies and private equity investors. I loved it.

The asset management industry has a great business model. Managers charge a fee based on the amount of money (assets) in the fund. Say it's one percent (that's high in the current environment, but it didn't use to be and it makes the math easier). One percent of a million dollars is ten thousand dollars. One percent of a billion dollars is ten million dollars.

Running a billion-dollar fund is only marginally more expensive than running a hundred million dollar one. So if you can grow the assets, the additional fees drop right to the bottom line. Hedge funds have even better economics for managers – higher fees and a cut of any profits. You can make a ton of money.

Lots of people have noticed this so there are plenty of funds out there. At year-end 2021, there were 8,887 open-end mutual funds and 2,690 ETFs, according to the Investment Company Institute (ICI), the trade group for the mutual fund industry. In a crowded market, getting visibility is important, and that's where public relations comes in. You have clients who manage money and track markets, you have media that write about markets and investing and the economy, and you have individuals and financial advisors who are looking for information and investment ideas. PR firms sit in the middle of this web, brokering news, information, and access to expertise.

The publishing community also saw dollar signs in the fund business. Dozens of new magazines and newsletters popped up in the 1980s, almost overnight, covering markets, investing, and retirement strategies. The daily newspapers added special mutual fund sections. CNBC was launched in 1989 in beautiful downtown Fort Lee, New Jersey to provide minute-by-minute coverage of the markets, much like sports reporting.

Public relations firms like mine work with clients to generate ideas that are intended to result in stories that portray the funds, and the fund managers, in a positive light. The cost of this – what the fund companies paid the PR firms – is a relative pittance compared to the fees generated by the successful managers. And the funds collected fees on the assets we helped them generate for as long as they kept the money. It was an unequal relationship but even so, it was a good business for us, too.

For individuals, there is plenty of advice to be had if you have enough money, or if you're young and look like you might have money In the future. But if you have less money, and fewer prospects, you're mostly ignored. Technology is providing a partial solution to this – lowering the costs for working with smaller investors. But technology alone can't solve the fundamental problem – getting individuals with no knowledge of the markets to save and invest. And, of course, these are the people who need that advice the most.

People in their sixties and seventies can only do so much to fix this. The one thing they need most (apart from money) is what they don't have: time. But there's hope for younger generations if we start now to dramatically re-think investing and retirement.

The good news is that it's in just about everyone's interest to find a solution. For the individual, more time means more money. For the asset managers more money means more fees. For the technology providers, younger investors mean consumers with a greater willingness to try new ideas. For everybody, it means moving away from reliance on pension plans and a Social Security system that can't possibly meet all its obligations and towards a more liberated life.

What say you, Bartleby?

CHAPTER THREE

What's in a Number?

401(K).

IT LOOKS LIKE WHAT IT is: a reference to an arcane subsection of Federal legislation, in this case the United States Revenue Act of 1978. it conjures the image of a dolorous bureaucrat with a green eyeshade and sleeve garters, a modern version of the scrivener

Bartleby, who after meeting with his motivational coach, was briefly energized to sneak in something a little extra into the bill in deference to the working man – a way for employees to set aside a few dollars for retirement on a pre-tax basis.

No big deal. Three years later, in 1981, the Internal Revenue Service issued new rules that let employees fund a 401(k) through payroll deductions. Over the next two years the idea took off, with nearly half of all big companies offering or thinking about offering a plan. As of 2018, more than 54 million Americans had some kind of participation in a 401(k). By early 2020 these plans held around $5.6 trillion, or about 20% of all US retirement assets.

Establishing these plans was not necessarily an act of altruism, however. Their adoption was coincident with a decline in traditional pensions, known as Defined Benefit (DB) plans, which had become a major part of the corporate landscape post-World War II.

DB plans were a perk offered employees and the responsibility of the employer to pay for and manage. They provided an income in retirement based on some kind of formula: years worked, salary and lifetime earnings, or seniority, for example. The company set aside the money to cover the costs and hired professional money managers to oversee the assets, matching the liabilities (the pensions owed) to the assets (the money in the plan to meet those obligations). Retirees were paid out of the assets in the plan.

It had the benefit of certainty — the retirees had guaranteed income for life, theoretically, at least (and part of the money was backed by a quasi-government entity, the Pension Benefit Guaranty Corp). All they had to do was cash the checks. But it was expensive to the employer.

As the US saw its post-war economic hegemony challenged, and corporations faced competition from around the globe, they looked for ways to save money. DB plans were an obvious candidate. With the advent of the defined contribution plan, there was a clear out – shift the responsibility for saving and investing to the individual.

Just how radical this idea would prove to be wasn't fully recognized at the time, least of all by those most directly affected - the millions of employees who suddenly became responsible for funding their own retirements. And not just setting aside the money, though that would be hard enough —managing it. This completely upended the individual's relationship to retirement.

The truth was that very few people would have the ability to save enough to fund a decent post-work life. They would have to rely on the magic of compounding — the growth of money over time, money itself generating more money. How, and how fast, that money compounded would depend on the investment choices they made.

An industry had grown up to compete for the trillions of dollars in DB plans, and that industry would compete for DC assets, too. In both instances, their interests aligned with growing the pile. There was a lot of good about this, and some not so good. Not everyone who was eligible participated. Smaller businesses, which employ nearly half the work force, around 60 million people, were inclined to opt out, due to the cost and complexity of setting up a program.

The smaller the business the less likely they are to offer retirement benefits. While 73% businesses with 50-99 employees offered some kind of retirement plan, that number falls to 28% for businesses with fewer than 10 employees. Only one out of three self-described "entrepreneurs" has a plan for themselves.

The plans were less than perfect. Not everyone matched the employees contributions, an important incentive to encouraging participation. Early on they were almost always "opt-in" meaning the employee had to choose to participate. For all too many, like Bartleby, it was easier to "prefer not." There was a mismatch of incentives inherent to the plans (and to any kind of savings) whereby younger people, in the early phases of their careers and already straining to make ends meet, were asked to take a further hit to take home pay to save for some ill-defined future. And for hourly workers, with less earnings upside, the challenge was that much greater.

There were other issues. It was unnecessarily difficult to move the assets if you changed jobs and, maybe, too easy to borrow against any accumulated savings, throwing sand in the gears of compounding. Too many participants opted for the more conservative investment options, including money market-like instruments such as stable value funds.

All this left many people on the outside looking in or with less than optimal portfolio allocations. And every year the clock was ticking.

A really useful engine.

CHAPTER FOUR

"I just want to feel useful"

THOSE ARE THE WORDS OF our friend, who lives around the corner out here in the country. Her 19th century farmhouse has a wood burning stove, Che Guevara posters on the wall, and, on the bookshelf, an Academy Award that she received for her 1992 documentary film, *The Panama Deception*.

A lifelong social activist, she once stood at the center of the revolution, a heady experience but not an especially lucrative one. In accepting her award from the Academy she gave what she describes as the "longest speech on record. The screen that tells you when your time is up ran out of warnings. By the time I looked down it was just snow. The orchestra, which is supposed to start up and drown you out, refused to play." In solidarity, she suggests, with a fellow unionist.

The Academy Award, when it came, was helpful and opened the door to new opportunities, including speaking at colleges around the country. But eventually that string ran out, and she returned to Chapel Hill in North Carolina. The years passed by. Her world is smaller now and a lot less busy than she would like. Like a lot of older Americans, she has been shuffled off towards the margins of society.

Those six words – "I just want to feel useful" – could be the rallying cry of much of the Baby Boom generation. Our kids blame us for destroying the planet, running up the national debt, and bankrupting Social Security. ("OK, Boomer.") Sure, there's some truth to that. But we've also been hammered by globalization and by the end of the post-war economic dominance enjoyed by our parents' generation. We've been downsized, outsourced, prematurely sent packing by employers. We've been made to feel, in the words of our friend, no longer useful.

But out where we live it's still all about self-sufficiency. One thing you can say about those old hippies: they manage to keep beer in the refrigerator, even if the refrigerator is on the front porch and there's no electricity. It's in the American tradition.

So, in its way, is the defined contribution plan. But to date it hasn't been really thought of that way. It's seen as a burden, a nuisance, an afterthought. While about 60% of working Americans have access to a 401(k) plan, only 32% invest in one and the median balance is just a little more than $22,000. Most people are outside the system entirely. This is unfortunate.

The reality is we're not going back to the old ways. No new DB plans are being started and the old ones are rapidly shutting down or converting to DC. Today, just 17% of private sector workers have access to a defined benefit plan, according to the Bureau of Labor Statistics. Public pension funds are still out there, and they are essentially DB plans, but most are woefully underfunded and will never be able to meet their promised obligations. To take an extreme example, New Jersey's state pension plan holds about $80 billion in assets against $212 billion in liabilities. The annual budget for the state is around $40 billion, so it would have to dedicate every tax dollar raised for three years just to bring the plan into balance.

You can argue about how this happened – there's plenty of bipartisan blame to go around – but the fact is public employees will almost certainly get stiffed. Social Security is in as bad a shape or worse, but the hole there is so deep that serious people despair of any kind of fix and everyone else just looks the other way and hopes the whole thing will just go away.

It will eventually come back into balance, but not in a way that will make anyone happy. As economist Herbert Stein put it in "Stein's Law" – "something that can't go on forever won't."

Why should I care?

CHAPTER FIVE

Different kinds of money

A YEAR OR SO AGO there was a piece on NPR discussing suicide among older Americans. A psychiatrist was interviewed as part of the segment. "The question I get asked the most," she said, "is why should anyone care? These people are old. They're going to die anyway."

I don't remember that she offered a compelling defense.

Growing up I figured suicide was a rare occurrence. You heard about it now and then but when it happened it was generally kept quiet. There was a lot of shame, a sense of failure, and of course the tragedy of a life cut short. But it turns out this isn't as unusual as we were taught to believe and, as anyone who's been paying attention knows, it's been getting worse.

There were 47,000 suicides in the U.S. in 2017 and those 65 and up accounted for more than 8,500 of them, according to the Centers for Disease Control and Prevention. Adults 85 and older, regardless of gender, are the second most likely age group to die from suicide. , there were 47.8 million people over the age of 65 in the U.S. as of 2015. By 2060, that number is expected to grow to 98.2 million. On current trends, that's a lot of people offing themselves.

There are many reasons for this, but failing health, loneliness, money, and despair are at the top of the list. Of those nearly 48 million Americans over 65, 12 million, or one in four, live alone. This isn't necessarily a function of poverty – other factors are at work, too – but being poor doesn't help and forces choices on retirees they don't want to have to face.

Money alone can't fix everything, but it does solve the problem of not having enough money. And money is a common link connecting many of these troubles. But not all money is the same. Social

Security is helpful, but it requires nothing more of the recipient than to put the check in the bank. Money that's been put away by families and individuals in self-directed investment accounts is different. It demands attention. It needs oversight. It draws you into the world. It encourages engagement and, through that, independence.

Money is just a tool, but a useful one, and it has a wonderful way of concentrating the mind. So that while not everyone will be launching a hedge fund anyone can buy shares in an exchange-traded fund (ETF) for a few dollars. All of a sudden you have a rooting interest – in stocks, in the economy, in the future. And the cost of ownership for the biggest of these funds is approaching zero.

There are tools available to accomplish this: low cost funds and automated savings vehicles that shuttle money into an investment program a few dollars at a time. Anyone with access to a smart phone or a computer can participate. The problem is not availability, it's education. To people making thirty or forty thousand dollars a year, saving five or ten dollars a week may seem pointless. But it's not. Time is a great multiplier. Compounding is a force of nature.

We have to learn to think about money differently – not just as a medium of exchange but as a vehicle for intellectual engagement through saving, investing, and, ultimately, spending.

If Social Security is going to run out of money, and it is, we have to find another way. Reaching those convinced they can't save requires a new way of thinking. It's important to understand that you don't have to be rich to have money in the stock market. You don't have to make a lifetime study of Fibonnaci signals, or the Elliott Wave Theory. All you need is a willingness to learn, some loose change, and the ability to stick with it.

Old age, poverty, and loneliness are inextricably linked. We can't fix old age, and years spent dithering over Social Security have put any kind of comprehensive solution out of reach. But that doesn't mean we can't do something.

Think of investing as a kind of tai chi for the balance sheet. It probably won't turn your grandmother into Arnold Schwarzenegger but it does offer improvement on the margin. And the exercise itself is almost beside the point. It's getting engaged that matters. Having access to even a little discretionary income – income they generate through their own investments – can help bring older people out of their heads, out of the house.

It's a different kind of money.

Gearing up.

CHAPTER SIX

Gearing

JAMES GRANT, A ONE-TIME columnist for the investment magazine, Barron's, and the founder of the eponymous *Grant's Interest Rate Observer*, has described money as the "distillation of labor." Of course, some forms of labor distill money at a higher rate than others.

At the low end are the more repetitive tasks that require hard work but minimal skill – dish washing, ditch digging, that sort of thing. At the other end are what might be called "rent-seeking" occupations: tasks that require no physical labor but that are privileged in our economic system and highly profitable. These are, not surprisingly, often jobs that are themselves about money. They are built around some kind of intellectual property, either individual or institutional. That may be an educational credential, or a particular skill, like a gift for mathematics.

Apart from the job requirements, a major difference in the two sets of occupations is "leverage," or, more colorfully, what the British call "gearing." Gearing is the ability to add revenues without adding a proportional amount of overhead. The higher the gearing, the bigger the profits. Traditional banks loan money and make a few percent on their capital. The biggest banks have trillions of dollars in capital so a few percent can add up. Financial advisors counsel individuals and families on investment and retirement strategies, and these days usually charge based on the amount of money they manage for the client. A common fee is one percent. Hedge funds were historically built around a "two and twenty" model - a 2% management fee and 20% of the profits. In all of these cases, the bigger the pile the bigger the fees collected.

A manual laborer has only his or her time and labor to sell. There may be a market for it that allows for the price of those services to be bid up, but there's only so much time in the day. The same is true for higher skill, judgement-based professions like lawyering.

Even if you charge $1,000 an hour, there are only so many hours. Gearing up here means adding more people, but more people also add costs. An enterprise like this will only be so profitable no matter how big it gets. It can never get out of low gear.

We tend to look at money as if it has some kind of mystical properties, but in reality it's nothing more than a medium of exchange. Grant's 1992 book, *Money of the Mind,* was mostly about the zaniness of the junk bond market in the late 1980s, but it also highlighted the notional nature of what's known as "fiat" currency. It begins with a true story about a financial advisor who holds a press conference in his front yard and offers to buy the retailer Dayton-Hudson for $6.8 billion. As it turns out, the man and his firm are light (short) about $6.7 billion.

When asked by a reporter if this is a hoax, the man replies, "I don't know. It's no more of a hoax than anything else. An offer is really an intangible thing." His lawyer later seeks to clarify, "This is a medical story, not a financial story."

Medical or financial, it raises a basic question: what's a dollar worth, and, equally important, who gets to say? The reality is that it's worth whatever someone will give you for it. A hedge fund manager client once told me with regards to his investment philosophy, "There are two things that matter: what'd you pay and what'd you get." What that same asset might be worth to someone else doesn't matter.

The current generation has been introduced to this concept by the rise of digital currencies. The dollar, at least, has a history of once being grounded in something of enduring value – gold. Bitcoin has been conjured out of nothing, and its volatility so far has made it a poor medium of exchange. Trading in Bitcoin is like living in a country with 500% inflation one day and 400% deflation the next. If you're selling something tangible —a loaf of bread, for instance— how do you price it? Every transaction becomes a speculation.

Bitcoin, Ethereum and the others have served to jumpstart thinking on more traditional currencies, too, none of which can stand up to too much critical examination. Like that client implied, the dollar, the euro, the yen, the yuan have value only to the extent we believe they have value. Their utility, for the moment at least, is that we all agree they can be exchanged for other goods, and the rate of exchange that we've agreed upon doesn't change too much day to day.

There's something else that has general agreement: money is good at producing more money, if you let it. This is broadly known as "compounding." Investing in a rising asset – or one that pays a dividend or interest – generates more money. That money, in turn, can itself be reinvested to generate more money. Cash on cash. But money is also good at costing us money. This is known as borrowing, and interest.

With borrowing you pay to use someone else's money. If you can make more on that money than you pay to borrow it, that's great. Eventually you can give the other person (or the bank) that money back and keep the difference. If, on the other hand, you use that money to buy something that declines in value (a new iPhone, for example), and you have to keep paying that person for the use of the money, you will find yourself poorer as a result of the transaction. The money has *cost* you money, and the money you spend on interest will be paying dividends to somebody else.

This is an obvious but important distinction, and it's the difference between having savings in old age and dying broke. Money can work for you, or it can work against you. And there's one more critical point to keep in mind: gearing up is not just for rich people. Anybody can do it.

"My fellow Americans ..."

CHAPTER SEVEN

It's all about Democracy

***BREAKER MORANT* WAS A 1980** film from Australian new wave director Bruce Beresford about a real-life trial that took place in South Africa during the second Anglo-Boer War. The war pitted the Dutch against the English for control of the country and its mineral wealth. The Germans were also involved and sided with the Dutch.

Morant and four others are accused of war crimes, including the assassination of a German missionary. They mount a precursor to what would later come to be known as the "Nuremburg Defense" – just following orders. Heading into the trial there's an exchange between Lord Kitchener, commander in chief of the British forces in the country, and Major Charles Bolton, the prosecutor.

"Needless to say, the Germans couldn't give a damn about the Boers," says Kitchener, referring to the ongoing maneuvering for post-war political advantage. "(It's) the diamonds and gold of South Africa they're after."

"I see, sir," Major Bolton replies. "They lack our altruism."

Lord Kitchener's eyebrows arch nearly out of the frame.

This is to say that possibly some skepticism is in order when a new stock brokerage firm comes along offering the ability to trade stocks for "free" as part of the long-running effort to "democratize" investing. The idea of democratizing as it's used here is to reduce transaction costs and enhance convenience, making markets and investment more accessible to more people. So far, so good. A noble enterprise.

This has, in fact, been going along for decades, at least since 1975 when stock trading commissions were deregulated, opening the door to the discount brokerage industry, and to then-upstarts like San Francisco-based Charles Schwab. Wall Street being Wall Street, the move to popularize trading is not quite the selfless enterprise it seems, however. It is not strictly about giving the little guy a break, though that has undeniably been one of its benefits.

You see this over and over again in the history of investing, with fixed trading commissions, with packaged investment products like unit trusts, mutual funds, and exchange-traded funds, and, more recently, with trading individual stocks. The cost of all these has gravitated, over time, towards "free." All are almost there now in one form or another, as far as the average individual investor is concerned.

Of course nothing is really free; there are still costs, but in these cases they haven't just been shifted or hidden they really have fallen, sometimes a lot. Writing on the 40th anniversary of what became known as "May Day", Wall Street Journal reporter Jason Zweig noted that prior to the changes an individual buying 100 shares of a $25 stock would have paid "a minimum commission of $49 and a bid-ask spread (the difference between the selling price and purchase price as determined by the broker/dealer) of $13." The bill: 2.5% of the $2,500 transaction. Hard to get ahead when you're being nicked like that.

Prior to deregulation, fixed commissions had been the rule on the NYSE for more than 180 years, a circumstance that seemed just fine to the house side of the business. James Needham, chairman of the NYSE at the time, famously predicted that negotiable commissions would bring "disaster to the majority." But it didn't and competition continued to drive the cost of stock trading lower and lower until it reached its logical conclusion: Robinhood Markets, Inc.

Robinhood opened its doors in 2013 and officially launched its trading app two years later at the LA Hacks hackathon. With the surge in Pandemic-related trading, it became the poster child for all that's good and bad about the younger generation of investors and speculators.

It is, in its way, just the next iteration of the "direct access" trading firms that were all the rage in the late 1990s and early 2000s. This technology had day traders crowding into trading rooms to lease computers and software that would allow them to transact directly with market makers at the exchanges, speeding transactions, cutting out the middleman.

It was a function of the rise of the Internet, which opened access to real-time price quotes and trading venues. It was coincident with, and helped drive, dot-com mania and pushed up both trading volume and the price of dot-com stocks. That mania resolved itself the way most Wall Street manias do: the market cratered. People lost lots of money.

Twenty years seems like about enough time to forget about all that. Milan Kundera wrote in *The Book of Laughter and Forgetting*, that the "struggle of man against power is the struggle of memory against forgetting." Something similar could be said about the madness of markets. But in this case we don't really work that hard to remember. More often, we embrace forgetfulness. Who, after all, wants to linger on that morning when their bank account was vaporized by short-dated, out-of-the-money GameStop options?

Robinhood trades are commission free and there are no account minimums. The app itself has been accused of "gamifying" markets, creating an unreality that makes losing money if not exactly fun, at least a good way to past the time while you're stuck in the house. The profile of the typical Robinhood client would seem to confirm that the torch has, indeed, passed to a new generation, and with it, the same opportunities that others have had to make a fortune or to self-immolate.

These people are, on balance, young with a median age of 31; half self-identify as first time investors, according to Vlad Tenev, the co-founder. (For insight as to where we are in the larger scheme of things, it's instructive to note that Tenev was testifying at a Congressional hearing when he said this, usually an end of cycle phenomenon.) The median Robinhood customer account size was just $240, the average $5,000. As of the end of 2020, about 13 percent of customers traded basic options contracts (e.g., puts and calls), something Tenev seemed to feel was unremarkable. But most customers, Tenev said, were investing in ETFs and listed stocks.

Robinhood was perhaps already working its way up the SEC's "things to do" list when GameStop came along. To be fair, the brokerage was just the execution platform of choice for the merry band of WallStreetBets traders hanging about on Reddit. Still, when the stock ran up from $20 a share in January to intraday highs of more than $450 in February, all for no particular reason (as Matt Levine at Bloomberg likes to say), Robinhood was forced to briefly suspend trading, casting a possibly unwelcome spotlight on the company. When the dust settled, some had made a fortune on the stock (Roaring Kitty); others, including professionally managed hedge funds, found themselves on the wrong side of all that . A significant and vocal minority was upset that trading had been halted. The political establishment worked itself into high dudgeon.

It's a brave new world when the term "paying for order flow" is suddenly running through the halls of Congress like so many costumed insurrectionists. Put simply, this means that someone is paying someone else for the opportunity to execute a trade. (It's more complicated than that, but that's the gist of it.) Harkening back to Zweig's piece, the buyers of this order flow are hoping to make money mostly on the bid/ask spread, but in this case it's pennies, or fractions of pennies, not dollars. This doesn't always work, but it works often enough for big wholesale trading firms like Citadel to be enthusiastic buyers of retail order flow.

It's easy to get lost in the weeds here in what's known broadly as "market structure", the Wall Street equivalent of "how a bill gets made." "Best execution" is an SEC requirement that brokers provide the most favorable transaction terms available to all customers. It sounds great but it's a moving target in an electronic marketplace. (Is "best" the lowest price or the fastest execution, for example? Those two aren't always the same.) Likewise, the idea of "price improvement" – that your broker will deliver a narrower bid/ask spread than what you see on your screen when you place your trade.

All this adds up to fractions of pennies to individuals, but tens of millions of dollars at scale. But as Heisenberg discovered with position and momentum, there's uncertainty in the trading process, too. Like Florida election results, the closer you look the more everything scatters, defying precision. Nonetheless the terminology has entered the lexicon, the market structure debate has found its way into the mainstream, and the promise of price improvement is now the subject of Schwab ads on CNBC.

Changes in market structure aside, there is still a cost and somebody is paying it. For the investor, there are two questions to ask: first, do you know what you're really paying (and do you care)? Second, all in, is this a cheaper way to transact than other options?

As always, there's a vocal coterie who believe individuals need to be protected from themselves (see Ocasio-Cortez, Alexandria). Oddly enough, those interests, which generally come from the left, often line up nicely with those of the right-leaning incumbents. Regulation tends to favor rent seekers.

There's an established progression for this sort of thing in the financial services world. Entrepreneur comes up with new idea. Wall Street (and regulators) decry the risk this poses. Entrepreneur perseveres, begins attracting customers. Established firms move to co-op the business model. The little guy, mostly a bystander in the fight, wins big, at least when it comes to cost and access.

Over time, market dynamics have gravitated in favor of lower costs and higher volume, as newer generations of technology have come online. App-based Robinhood falls squarely in that progression. As we've noted, this has opened the door to small investors who really can put money to work in the market; those $250 Robinhood accounts are evidence of that. You can then take that $250 and (as of February 26, 2021) buy 0.7 shares of an S&P 500 ETF like the Vanguard 500 Index Fund (VOO). Cost to trade: $0; expense ratio (what Vanguard subtracts annually to run the fund): 0.03% of the assets under management.

If historical trends persist, your money will grow along with corporate America, or on average about 8.0% a year. Not GameStop numbers, but a return that's several orders of magnitude more reliable.

Investing this way requires a certain discipline, first to put the $250 away and add to it, and second, to not drop it all on a non-fungible Kings of Leon token (NFT), or something similar. This is where critics have a point: just because you can trade meme stocks on margin 24-hours-a-day using your phone doesn't mean you should.

Democracy.

Roll the bones.

CHAPTER EIGHT

A random walk

BARBARA LIKES TO WALK DOWN THE MIDDLE OF JO Mac Road. It's not that busy and it doesn't go anywhere. The road and its tributaries wander off to eventually dead end in the low slung Orange County hills, among the loblolly pines, the hardwoods, the occasional mobile home. Besides, nearly everyone who has a reason to be driving on Jo Mac knows her, and they all slow down to say hello.

She has lived on this road for more than 20 years. She is, as they say, beloved.

She's a fan of organic food, of solar power, and is skeptical of governments, big business, and, more recently, big healthcare, pretty standard fare for this part of the world. She has provided a home for a multitude of Woofers and other dreamers who, hypothetically you understand, believed they, too, would like to live in a drafty 19th century house heated by a wood-burning stove and grow their own food.

Is that enough for a life? Did she make enough films, organize enough rallies to bend the moral arc of the universe ever so slightly? No doubt she has touched a lot of souls. Both the wider world and the small bore domain of Jo Mac are better for her being here.

Some of the locals might not care for all of Barbara's politics if they stopped to think about it: the time spent in the Central American jungles, the documentaries exposing the inanities of U.S. policy there. They probably haven't heard the story about how she met David Kasper on a cross country caravan to New York City in support of the United Nations Second Special Session on Disarmament in 1982, how they would become partners in the film-making business. How one thing led to another, the way these things do, and 11 years later they were on the stage together at the Academy Awards.

But they like her and that's all that matters. They fetch wood and bring food. Cut the grass. They inquire about her health which has lately not been as good as it was. Towards the end of 2020, she was diagnosed with stage three colon cancer. She had surgery, then researched and agonized over whether or not to follow that up with chemo long enough to render the option moot.

"Decision by procrastination," I suggested one day when we were out walking.

Based on our present understanding of the science, a lot of cancers appear random. You don't smoke, you don't live on top of a chromium dump or next to a nuclear power plant. You eat organic. You've done what you can. The rest is a crap shoot.

How do you live in the face of this uncertainty? In his podcast, *How to Tickle Yourself*, the writer Duff McDonald advances the viewpoint of the Boddhisatva: the future doesn't exist, probability is an illusion and figuring the odds is a waste of time.

Others differ on this. In his book, *A Drunkard's Walk*, Leonard Mlodinow writes about the history of probability and how, in his words, it "rules our lives." His point, simply put, is that we make certain assumptions based on our experiences. Many of these assumptions are wrong. We see patterns where none exist, and fail to correctly calculate the likelihood of any particular outcome. Things we think are wildly improbable happen with some regularity, and vice versa. Luck, defined as the favorable intersection of random events, is a bigger factor in our lives than many of us care to admit.

Not surprisingly, many probability pioneers were also gamblers.

Having money at stake is always clarifying, and there are those whose lives, and livelihoods, depend on the correct calculation of the odds. Casinos, for one, run on probability. In "Starting from Scratch," a 2020 episode of the radio show, *This American Life*, producer Mary Beth Kirchner follows the fortunes of a part-time Las Vegas limo driver named Joe ("please don't use my last name"). Joe's goal is to end up every day with more money than he began with. "One time I started out with $32 and ended up with $84,000," he tells Kirchner. He does this not by driving the limo, but by periodic forays into the casinos to play blackjack.

A professional acquaintance of Joe offers this insight. "He is by no means dishonest. He's an opportunist. He's the kind of guy that if there's a dollar to be made, he'll make ten." This view is confirmed by, among others, Joe's daughter ("please don't use my first or last name"), whom Joe raised as a single parent. "We would walk in (to the casinos) and everyone would know him," she says. She remembers both the good times and the not so good. "Sometimes we had to search for quarters on the floor," she says.

George, a Las Vegas casino pit boss ("please don't mention my full name or where I work"), adds, "I see the numbers. There's not a player in this place or any casino I've ever been who made more than they lost." Possibly George's experience proves nothing, possibly his experience is itself random, but it is seconded by the fact of Las Vegas itself.

In a different book about a more singular set of variables, *A Random Walk Down Wall Street*, Princeton economics professor Burton Malkiel also grapples with uncertainty, in his case the behavior of markets.

Investors, like punters, have contrived all manner of systems to game the world in which they operate. In markets, these systems and their practitioners can be identified variously as chartists (those who create graphs of stock prices or other factors and look for recurring patterns over time), momentum players (buying shares of stock that are going up on the theory that they will keep going up), fundamentalists (valuations based on discounted cash flows), Smart Beta, and Risk Parity, among others. There is a colorful agglomeration of theories: Elliott Wave, Dow, Relative Strength, Efficient Market, Modern Portfolio. There is the academically blessed study of Behavioral Economics and its corollary, Behavioral Finance, for which lead acolyte Richard Thaler won the Nobel Prize in 2017.

Malkiel runs through them all, concluding that they are essentially worthless for the simple reason that "past movements in stock prices cannot be used reliably to foretell future movements." Score one for Duff.

The distribution of health and of sickness may not be entirely random but, like markets, it's impossible to predict. Knowing that a 65-year-old-male has a 60% chance of living to 80 is good, but it doesn't say anything about you. As Duff might say, possibly the entire concept of probability is an illusion, a mathematical construct.

As a spiritual matter, that may be correct; as a guide for monastery living it is doubtless a useful insight. As a framework for retirement planning it's not especially helpful. We have to make certain assumptions about longevity and the performance of markets. "I long ago came to the conclusion that all life is 6 to 5 against," says a Damon Runyon character in the story, "*A Nice Price*," and, for planning purposes, that seems about right.

There are areas where everyone can agree. In a discussion of dice-throwing, Mlodinow asks, "What does it mean, from a practical point of view, when we say the chances are 1 in 6 a die will land on two? If it doesn't mean that in any series of tosses the die will land exactly on the two exactly one time in six, then on what do we base our belief that the chances of throwing a two are really one in six?"

It's a good question, and precisely the one Barbara faced when trying to decide whether or not to undergo chemotherapy for her cancer. In her case, the oncologist laid out the following scenario: assume ten people with stage three colon cancer. They have the same surgery. All will be offered the option of chemotherapy. Seven of those would be fine without it. Of the remaining three, two will get no benefit and the cancer will return, and one will have her life extended by some number of years.

But there is no way to know the outcome for you. Weighed against this is the 100% certainty that you're 74-years-old and that chemo will make you sick, and may have long-lasting side effects.

Barbara looked at these odds and decided to pass.

A pivotal moment in Mlodinow's book is his discussion of Jakob Bernoulli and the "Law of Large Numbers." Developed in the early 18th century, this idea is formally stated as follows: "as the number of identically distributed, randomly generated variables increases, their sample averages approach their theoretical average." In other words, with enough repetitions the odds, whatever they may be, will assert themselves. That is the essence of probability, and of Las Vegas.

Because our own sample set will always be limited, most of us prefer to operate on a more intuitive principle: the Law of Small Numbers. This, however, is almost certain to lead to many wrong turns in life, and in the markets.

Health is random. Wealth, in its inherited form, is, too. Markets, as Malkiel has noted, behave unpredictably over the short term. Fads come and go. Does value outperform growth? Sometimes. Will small cap beat large? Depends on what period you measure. Can chartists predict the future? Sure, if it looks more or less like the recent past.

Throw the bones.

What's to be made of all this? Mlodinow's most helpful insight may come from a Venn-diagram-like musing on the practical applications of theory. "Successful people in every field are almost universally members of a certain set – the set of people who don't give up," he writes.

Work hard enough, long enough, and something will happen. You just don't know what or when. It might or might not be good. Getting to the most probable outcome is a law of large numbers problem; getting any old outcome is just flipping a coin. The best way to improve the chances of getting the outcome you want is to flip a lot of coins.

For investors, this is useful in a very specific way. The likelihood of getting a positive return on your investment goes up the longer you invest. From 1926 to the present – not quite Bernoulli's *Infinite Series* but the best we've got – stocks have had a positive return in every rolling 15-year period. This includes those periods spanning the Great Depression, Black Monday, the Dot Com bust, the Financial Crisis, and the Great Cessation. The investing equivalent of flipping a lot of coins is holding a diversified portfolio over time.

We're all on a random walk. For Mlodinow, that journey is defined by the laws of probability. For Duff, who declines to acknowledge the existence of time, this calculated approach is meaningless. For, Malkiel markets hold a certain truth but we have to be patient to uncover it. For those struggling with life and death decisions, like Barbara, it can all come down to the toss of a coin. If they're lucky, they will find themselves on a long run of "heads." Or, maybe not.

Who knew?

CHAPTER NINE

There's a theory

THERE IS A THEORY THAT THE WORLD AND ITS money are changing. The currencies in this new land will be Bitcoin, or meme stocks, NFTs, or maybe Nike pumps.

To this latter point, early in 2021 long-time senior Nike executive Ann Herbert suddenly found herself kicked to the curb after Bloomberg reported that her 19-year-old son, going by the moniker of "West Coast Joe", was moving major sneaker merch – buying and reselling hundreds of thousands of dollars worth of shoes every month on the secondary market.

First, who knew there was a secondary market in never-worn basketball shoes? Who buys these? Second, what? Hundreds of thousands of dollars a month?

Bloomberg wrote that "ultra-rare shoes such as the Air Jordan 1 OG Dior—a collaboration between Nike and the Parisian fashion house that was limited to 8,500 pairs—have become 'grails' worth $10,000 or more."

West Coast Joe told the Bloomberg reporter that, "... the night the stimulus checks hit (last May) my sales tripled. We did $600,000 worth of business." Good to know all that government money isn't going to waste. Still, as a medium of exchange sneakers do have a few drawbacks. Most obviously, you can only wear one pair at a time, so if you're planning to trade them for a cup of coffee or a new Tesla you have to keep a spare at the ready.

But the thought is that younger generations will no longer be bound by what the ancients had decreed would be a storehouse of value – gold, of which there is only so much, or dollars, the supply of which is apparently infinite. New things will have value as assigned to them by such monetary authorities as Wallstreetbets. This includes not just shoes, but Non-Fungible Tokens (NFTs) – a digital store of information that exists on the blockchain. Dollars are fungible, one is as good as another; NFTs are unique, but only in a very narrow sense.

The poster child for this particular bit of insanity so far has been the sale by Christie's of a digital work by the artist known as Beeple for $69 million, the third-most expensive work ever sold by a living artist, according to the auction house. Not exactly a vault full of gold, or even an actual painting, it is nonetheless highly representative of ... something.

But there are other ideas out there for building wealth, including one that seems almost quaint: introducing high school students from economically disadvantaged backgrounds to investing in the stock market is one. Giving them real money to buy stuff. Building the case for long-term investing by trotting out all the usual pedagogical suspects: Einstein's likely apocryphal comment on the value of compounding, the hoary old example of having a million dollars versus a penny that doubles every day for a month.

The funny thing is, these things actually work. Even more surprising, the concept is being applied in the real-world by a group of college kids through a program known as First Generation Investors (FGI), started in 2018 at the University of Pennsylvania by Dylan Ingerman, Cole Mattux, and Alex Ingerman.

From a couple of high school kids in Philadelphia, FGI is now on the ground in 25 schools around the country, including Harvard, Columbia, and Vanderbilt as well as multiple historically black colleges and universities (HBCUs) like Morehouse and Spelman. At Duke in

Durham the chapter is headed by Niso Nahmiyas, a freshman. He heard about FGI soon after landing on campus and reached out to the founders in fall 2020. By the winter, he had a group up and running and had recruited other Duke students to act as tutors. He then began reaching to local high schools to enlist students in the program. Given the pandemic, and the inability to meet in person, it wasn't easy.

"I sent out about 500 emails to teachers and administrators," he says. Most of these just disappeared into the ether, but he did manage to land an opportunity to make a Zoom presentation to the Middle College High School at Durham Tech, a collaboration between the public school system and the local community college. Average family income at the school: $40,000, low even for Durham. Twenty kids signed up; ten were ultimately enrolled (the other ten were steered to programs at different schools).

The first session convened on a February Saturday at noon, via Zoom, in the midst of the meme investing madness. GameStop had been all over the news for months and Reddit Wallstreetbets all-star, Keith Gill, had his thirty seconds of government-issued fame, testifying before Congress two days earlier. Gill, who once worked in marketing for an insurance company, was sitting on some $30 million in meme stock trading profits. The week before, GameStop had traded as high as $52.66 and as low as $38.50. In January, the shares were going for about $350. By mid-March they would be back around $250. It was a tough time to talk long-term investing.

Bloomberg's Matt Levine has a theory that, during the Pandemic lockdown, day trading became one of the few forms of entertainment available to Gen Z'ers and Millennials stuck at home. Hence, RobinHood could be more accurately seen as competing with Fortnite and Draft Kings than with Schwab or Fidelity. It was a videogame with real money. This may not have been all bad, however. Levine reasoned as follows:

"To the extent that YOLOing ("you only live once") options on Robinhood is a substitute for buying index ETFs, it is probably mostly bad for its customers. To the extent that YOLOing options on Robinhood is a substitute for buying, like, weed or lottery tickets, it is probably good for its customers' financial health. Especially if they get bored with options trading when pandemic lockdowns end, return to their everyday lives, and keep buying boring ETFs on Robinhood out of habit."

Niso puts it this way, "The best thing would be to make a million dollars in an hour, but we tell them that's not likely to happen. They're more likely to crash and burn. When that happens the program gives them something to fall back on."

Niso is himself only a few years removed from high school and his background is in some ways similar to that of those he's tutoring. He's a first generation American. His father is from Turkey, his mother, Colombia. But there are also differences. His parents both graduated from college and met while working at Morgan Stanley in New York City. He attended the Bronx High School of Science. He was exposed to finance from an early age.

Like the Ingermanns, like Cole, he is a believer in the power of markets. "The reason it's called First Generation Investors is because none of these kids' parents had the opportunity to learn what they're learning," he says. "The idea is to stop the cycle of some people having the opportunity to invest and take advantage of compounding and others working hard but never accumulating any wealth."

This latter group is forever living on the edge: one wrong turn and they're on their way to a spot next to Francis McDormand in the Walmart parking lot. That's not good for anybody.

The goal, too, is to bring people who've been alienated by capitalism back into the market economy by having them pay attention to something they would not have paid attention to before. "Just asking the kids to think about this stuff sends them off in a new direction," is how Niso puts it. That the sums involved were dwarfed by the money changing hands around AMF or GameStop didn't seem to matter that much.

"I worried that given the small amount of money they might lose interest, but they were mostly happy to just have a stake in the game," says Niso. This won't work for everyone everywhere, but neither does anything else. The program is already starting to show results, and not just in the stock market. There's the kid in Philadelphia who walked miles through the winter cold to get to an investment class inspired by FGI (back when it was possible to meet in person). Three kids at the Harvard chapter wrote about it in their college essays, and ended up going to Harvard. The same thing with two kids at Syracuse and one at Georgia Tech. Lives are being changed.

FGI's first day's lesson is pretty basic stuff. A worksheet includes questions like "What is a stock?" and "What might make a company's stock go up or down?" It's a virtual class and on the computer screen where there is the usual assortment of bored looking teenage faces familiar to any high school teacher. The dress is Zoom casual: t-shirts, backwards baseball caps, hoodies. The lighting is mostly bad. Of the ten kids, five are black, two Hispanic, and three white. There are nine males, one female, a disparity they plan to address in future groups.

The conversation tends to lag the way it will with teenagers, but there's one kid who stands out. Asked what he knows about the market, he flags a stock that has been all over the place that week – up $100 here, down $100 there. Crazy, GameStop-like action. Interesting, but not a part of the core curriculum. Clearly, he's ready for the advanced class.

Others, though, are in a different place. For one, "knowing where the name Wall Street comes from" was the best part. (There was a real wall there once.) All in all, Niso is happy with the day's outcome. There are seven more weeks to bring everybody along. In week four, they start to get real money to invest. If they finish the program and graduate from high school, they get to keep the cash.

FGI started small, but it's growing fast. There are, it would appear, two big challenges. First, getting kids interested in long-term investing in an era of 100% daily returns, NFTs, and Nike sneaker trading and, second, keeping them interested once all these markets crash and lots of people go broke.

As in so many other areas of life, the Kardashian family can be counted on to provide useful insight here. In this case, a tweet sent out by Kylie Jenner, half-sister to the Kardashian clan, was used by Niso to illustrate the difference between idiosyncratic and market risk. About the messaging app Snapchat, she said in 2018, “Sooo does anyone else not open Snapchat anymore? Or is it just me … ugh this is so sad.” That sent the company’s stock tumbling, down 7% on the day, knocking $1.6 billion off the market cap.

Oddly, the broader market mostly shrugged off the younger Jenner’s negative Snapchat review, with the S&P 500 declining a modest -0.6% on the day, thus making Niso’s point. Clearly the Kardashians are an idiosyncratic risk.

A post-Keynesian paradise.

CHAPTER TEN

The First Gen Speaks

WE HAVE ESTABLISHED IN EARLIER CHAPTERS THAT THERE IS nothing special about money; since the abolition of the gold standard the U.S. currency has essentially been untethered and now exists as a kind of barter arrangement underwritten by the government and the Federal Reserve. Its value is something about which we all agree to agree. But in order for fiat currency like this to work, that value can't be seen as totally arbitrary.

Along comes Modern Monetary Theory (MMT) which takes the already fantastical process of valuing paper money to "11". By one definition, MMT is "a heterodox macroeconomic theory that describes currency as a public monopoly." As such, coin can be created at will by the government to serve the needs of the people, whatever they may be. True or not, there had been little to contradict this assertion (until recently).

MMT goes on to state that "unemployment is evidence that a currency monopolist is overly restricting the supply of the financial assets." Money is printed; prosperity ensues. Taxes are the tool used to manage inflation, sucking money out of the economy, reducing demand and driving prices down. Ipso facto: a post-Keynesian paradise.

Maybe so. There was a cartoon, published sometime around the year 2000, in which an old geezer chastises a newly minted dot-com millionaire who has wandered into his store. "You know, he says, these are all just castles made of sand. They'll be washed away the next time the tide comes in."

To which the dot-commer replies, "Wow! What an evocative metaphor. Well, I'm off to Tahiti."

Of course they both turned out to be right. Yes, billions of dollars of venture capital was flushed in the dot-com crash. Hundreds of companies disappeared. Thousands of people lost their jobs. On other hand, Tahiti is no doubt nice.

Bowdlerized versions of MMT now circulate through the public discourse like wooden nickels. More than a few appear to be rattling around in the pockets of certain members of Congress. It's a different kind of green New Deal, standing the historical relationship between wealth and productivity on its head. It's true that for the last 30 years or so (about the time MMT has been around) there has been little in way of consequences for printing money. So why not turn it up to 11? Build roads, bridges, a dome over the country to capture greenhouse gases. But just in case this turns out to have unforeseen consequences, it's good to have a backup plan. A regular job, maybe. An investment strategy, certainly.

Eighteen-year-old Eh Wei is a bit on the short side but solidly built, with the body of a weightlifter (which he is). He's also punctual, not a trait always associated with teenagers. It was Eh Wei who had asked about the meme stocks on that Saturday when the initial First Generation Investors (FGI) meeting convened via Zoom. On this occasion he is sitting outside (Covid) at a coffee shop on a hot summer day in Chapel Hill.

Unlike most of the students Eh Wei was already trading for his own account before the program began. Like the others in the class, he was the first in his family to do so. As a day trader, he says, he made some money, lost some money, a fairly typical experience. It was, he says, a way to learn. The family came to the U.S. from Myanmar by way of Thailand, fleeing persecution, when Eh Wei was three years old. Members of the Karen tribe, they had been driven from their homes by the Myanmar military in part of what has been called one of world's longest-running civil wars, a brutal cleansing of an ethnic minority that is ongoing.

Eh Wei and his family eventually ended up in North Carolina. In addition to his parents, there are five sisters. Eh Wei is the next to youngest. They are all making their way in their adopted land. His third eldest sister just graduated from nearby Guilford College and has plans to return to law school. Another has arranged for Eh Wei to work at a local nonprofit, the Refugee Community Partnership ("We envision a world where migration is seen as courageous and is met with the supportive community, safety, and healing necessary to rebuild home"). They work. They send money to family back in Myanmar. They move ahead.

Eh Wei himself is a thoughtful, soft-spoken young man with a newly minted citizen's sense of purpose. He has not been, I suspect, especially disillusioned by the revelation that the streets of his adopted hometown aren't paved with gold, and that some of them aren't paved at all.

"Labor is life," he says. By this he means, in part, that the historically nomadic existence of the Karen people has made it hard to accumulate much in the way of wealth. No one is sitting around the campfire clipping coupons. While this is an extreme example, it's a circumstance broadly familiar to millions of Americans: all too few can put their hands on a few hundred dollars in a pinch. There is an exhaustive supply of data on this, and it makes for a dreary read.

Sadly, the situation can't be solved by conjuring money out of thin air.

It may be that those who have seen the world's rougher side are quicker to understand this: they are possibly less given to magical thinking. Under these circumstances, the chance to learn investing is a potentially a life-changing experience, says Eh Wei. About FGI he says, "A lot of minorities want to get in the stock market but don't know how it works."

As much as there is a magic to the stock market, it is conjured through the power of compounding, a function of both earnings growth over time and reinvested dividends. Like others in the class, Eh Wei has seized on this idea, and that's reflected in his FGI portfolio which is built around positions in an S&P 500 ETF and the QQQ.

These are not get rich quick holdings, but they are a bet on the future. The triple Q is an index-tracking mutual fund that trades like a stock and has an expense ratio – the annual cost of ownership – of 0.2%, or $2 for every $1,000 invested. Not nothing by present day standards but well below the average cost for an actively managed mutual fund where fees generally average from 0.5% to 1.0%. It has as its top ten holdings a who's who of megacap tech stocks, including Apple, Microsoft, Alphabet, Amazon, and Tesla.

The S&P 500 ETF basically captures the return of the broad stock market. "VOO," Vanguard's category offering, has an expense ratio of 0.03%, or 30 cents per thousand dollars. Cheap.

Holders of both – but of the triple Q especially – did well over the five-year period ending in 2021: VOO more than doubled while the triple Q tripled. None of this came in a straight line, however. Over that period, QQQ shares have traded for as little as $114 in 2016 and as high as $381 in 2021. They lost more than 25% in about a month during the spring 2020 sell off. Volatile but not crazily so. No diamond hands needed.

Countries that have tried to solve their budget problems by printing money have faired poorly, though none have been as big as the United States or played such a central role in the global economy. Venezuela, Zimbabwe, and Argentina are three that have gone this route in modern memory, followed by hyperinflation and economic collapse. The latter, amusingly, once saw one of its naval vessels seized at a Ghanaian port by a hedge fund and a gaggle of bankruptcy lawyers, the result of a decade-long dispute over a billion dollar loan.

In times like these, Adam Smith's tweedy remark that "there's a great deal of ruin in a nation" tends to get a lot of play. It may be that this will not go so well here either, though the "great deal" threshold is probably higher. Still, strange things can happen when the numbers no longer add up as we have seen. Go get the wheelbarrow.

As part of a March class exercise Eh Wei reported on Johnson & Johnson (JNJ). "I looked at the chart," he said. "It's been pretty much linear (heading up) all year." Though purchasing individual stocks is not part of the program, his timing was good. JNJ closed the day before at around $156; by August it was trading at $175, up more than 10% over the five months, not including dividends, and better than 20% annualized. "It's a life changing experience, investing," says Eh Wei.

It can be. It was Jim Grant, scourge of financial alchemists everywhere, who once wrote that in the long run in America the buyers have been right and the sellers have been wrong. MMT and other fantastical notions aside, that optimism is still at the core of the American experience. Eh Wei would be a buyer.

Could you repeat that?

CHAPTER ELEVEN

Squawk in the school hall

BRETT OSLON TEACHES AP HISTORY AND FINANCIAL LITERACY AT Motivation, a Title One high school in West Philadelphia. He estimates that about a third of the student body there is made up of "first generation students," including a large contingent from African countries like Ethiopia and Liberia.

Late one September Friday in 2019 he was alone in the school when the phone rang. On the other end of the line was a cold-calling student from the University of Pennsylvania named Blake Kernen (daughter of CNBC personality, Joe Kernen), asking to speak to the financial literacy teacher. She was calling on behalf of First Generation Investors (FGI).

"Having taught in Philadelphia for 21 years I thought I'd heard everything, but this was the first time I'd heard this pitch," says Oslon. "High school kids from impoverished areas are going to spend time with college kids talking about the stock market. And by the way they're going to give your students $100 to invest. It sounded too good to be true."

But Oslon listened. The following Saturday, he delivered 25 students for FGI's first ever class. Good grades were not a prerequisite. We were looking for kids with a "spark," says Oslon. This is consistent with the program's overall philosophy. "We don't look at grades because we realize that the interest for something like this isn't tied to how they do in school," says FGI's co-founder Cole Mattox.

Oslon likes to tell the story of two students who were late to class one day, talking in the hall. "Our principal was upset that they were late but when I spoke with them I found out they were having a Squawk Box-like conversation about the value of compounding," Oslon says. "One of them said something like 'this compounding is insane.' Both kids are in college now."

That life is not fair will come as a surprise to no one who's paying attention. It is possible that fairness is not a quality inherent to the universe. It's possible that the obsession with it is mostly a distraction. Establishing fairness as a prerequisite to anything pretty much ensures it will never get done.

FGI essentially sidesteps this issue. You could say that it's built on the presumption that fairness would be great but it's a lot to expect. Here's something else to know. Markets are not fair, either. Some people know more than others. Some have faster connections to the exchanges. Some can afford to lay their own fiber optic cables from Chicago to New York to gain a fractional advantage in the timing of a trade.

The average individual can't compete with that. But they don't have to. Markets may not be fair to day traders, but they reward constancy and patience, qualities anyone can cultivate. It was Thomas Pynchon who observed that "If you get people asking the wrong questions you don't have to worry about the answers." Is it fair is the wrong question.

Efficient Market Theory holds that the price of a share of stock reflects all the available information at a given moment in time. Behavioral investing theorists suggest that excesses in sentiment can cause a dislocation in prices – too high or too low – and that pricing inefficiency can persist.

Known information can cause people to act in unpredictable ways. "Markets can stay irrational longer than you can stay solvent" is how

Wall Street sums this view up. Burton Malkiel, whom we've mentioned earlier, looked at all this and concluded that with the possible exception of a modest "small cap effect" there is no known way to consistently beat the averages.

This is not to say that there won't be people and strategies that outperform. In any random sample or time period there will always be outliers. It is to say, however, that those that outperform this year are unlikely to outperform the next (or the next). Further, it's impossible to anticipate who or what will do well. In that sense, maybe markets are fair. No one knows anything.

But there is one field that could use a little leveling and it's the one where FGI plays: educating people that markets exist. That while they may or may not be fair, they are fair enough.

If you're sixteen and want to hear about why you shouldn't run up credit card debt, then the current crop of financial literacy courses are for you. If you don't have a credit card and aren't expecting to take out a mortgage anytime soon you might strain to understand the relevance. You might, however, find the stock market interesting.

While the day to day action is mostly noise, it's engaging noise and some of it can be useful. The people involved are generally an interesting set – whether it's Hetty Green (known as the "Witch of Wall Street," she wandered the canyons of lower Manhattan in the late 19th century and died as one of country's richest women), Ivan Boesky and his briefcases full of cash or J.P. Morgan (the person, not the bank) bailing out the U.S. Government with $100 million in gold during the Panic of 1893. And there are higher minded folks as well – historians, philanthropists, public servants – a Tolstoyan universe of characters.

And there's a knock-on benefit: investing generally, and FGI specifically, can be a calling card for entry into a broader world, both current and historical. Students at Motivation have seen their families make the trip from East Africa to Southwest Philadelphia but the few blocks up the road to U. Penn can seem unimaginably far. FGI expands the possible.

Addressing the issue of social mobility is not really part of the FGI brief, but it's a non-trivial problem, and one the program's graduates will increasingly confront as they move along through life. Not everyone will get rich but those who continue to study the markets and invest will inevitably see their horizons expand to encompass a novel set of personages and ideas. It's a brave new world, but an alien one, and an easy place to get lost.

In her book *Moving Up Without Losing Your Way: The Ethical Costs of Upward Mobility*, Jennifer Morton, a professor of philosophy at the University of Pennsylvania, writes about the "ethical and emotional tolls paid by disadvantaged college students seeking upward mobility." By ethical she is referring to choices that lead to the kind of social dislocations that happen when a student (or anyone) moves across class lines – leaving behind friends and family and, in some cases, country and language.

As a nation of immigrants, Americans have long taken it for granted that these kinds of sacrifices are necessary. But people aren't coming here from Genoa in wooden ships so much anymore; the migration we are encouraging now is motivated by economics. As such, it seems strange to characterize these journeys as "ethical" choices as Professor Morton does; they aren't ethical as the term is generally understood. They involve ambition, an often inchoate desire to step out into a bigger world. And they most definitely involve choices.

But leave aside the book's semantics and the blather about "codeswitching" and the author's point is well taken – change is hard. You're not just going somewhere new; you're leaving something old behind. Those bobbing in your wake will continue to exert a heavy emotional toll, for good or ill. These people – friends, family, casual acquaintances you bump into on the street – will sometimes contrive, consciously or not, to hold back those Morton calls "strivers."

While this is true for everyone, it's also true that the further the distance travelled the greater the price exacted. So it's the economically disadvantaged who have the toughest trip – the kind of kids you find in the FGI program. There is a line in a P.G. Wodehouse novel about an individual who "becomes unhinged in the presence of too many spoons," meaning he was uncomfortable with a formal dinner table setting. That's funny, but it's also a real concern.

That this should be the case isn't fair either. Economic advancement shouldn't force a series of binary choices on the would-be striver, asking them to toggle between prosperity and alienation, but it often does. There's a term for this phenomenon of course, and it draws for inspiration from both ancient Eastern wisdom and Star Trek: Kobayashi Maru ("little wooden boat").

The concept of Kobayashi Maru made its debut in the 1982 film, *Star Trek II: The Wrath of Khan*. It references a training exercise designed as a test of character for leaders of the Star Fleet. In the film, starship captain James Kirk confronts a lose-lose proposition involving the Klingons, arch-enemies of his own Federation, and a Federation starship stranded in Klingon territory. Offered a choice of two alternatives – both of which end in disaster – the ever-resourceful Kirk opts for a third way: he reprograms the game to allow for success. Everyone is a winner.

You could think of this as cheating, but you could also see it as a "meta approach" to problem solving, similar to that suggested by Pynchon. Should your choices be limited by an artificially created framework? Why or why not? Discuss.

If your parents never finished high school, you might feel a little out of place rolling through the halls of Harvard or Princeton. You may feel, to again use Professor Morton's word, "inauthentic." But this creates a Kobayashi Maru-like false dichotomy. As Professor Morton puts it, "If authenticity is thought of as staying true to one's childhood self or a particular culture, then most education will be inauthentic." People don't grow up reading Plato or writing algorithms. These are learned behaviors.

At any rate, graduates of FGI are likely to confront their own version of the Star Trek test at some time in their lives. Continuing to invest and to build wealth will inevitably force a reconsideration of their place in the economic and social order. Not everyone from their past will be following the stock market, talking about CAPE ratios, or running around quoting Burton Malkiel. This will almost certainly be a small subset of their friends and acquaintances, leading them to feel out of place in both their old and their new lives.

To date, the program is too new to have encountered this issue at scale. So far, it's mostly been about moving up. So kids attending FGI's, kids in the U. Penn program have enrolled in U. Penn, kids at Georgia Tech have gone to Georgia Tech, and so on. Everything is good. But everything is no longer the same.

"There's a difference in who they are now and who they were before the program," says Oslon of his Motivation students. "Their majors have changed. They used to default into liberal arts. Now they're gravitating towards finance and computer science. They know what they want to do. They're on an upward trajectory. They know 'I can do this.'"

Tipping the scales.

CHAPTER TWELVE

Toting it up

MAN'S LIFE IS NOT A BUSINESS, SAID THE AUTHOR Saul Bellow. Put another way, one's daily comings and goings should not forever be toted up in a spreadsheet. Yet some math is required from time to time.

Capitalism is clear what it's about – creating wealth. Figuring out how to distribute that wealth falls to the political class. In recent decades we have done a good job with the former task but a poor one designating those charged with overseeing the latter. As a result, debate has arisen over the nature of the social contract and the value of capitalism itself. Money is not life; but money does have a say in how we live our lives. It can be used to cruise around on private jets. It can be put to work bringing clean water to remote African villages or supporting programs like FGI. It can sit around doing nothing.

It can also come and go. Markets can plunge without warning. In 1987 stocks dropped more than 20% in a single day. The 2001 Dot Com collapse saw the Nasdaq fall nearly 80%. In the 2007-2008 Financial Crisis the value of the S&P 500 was cut in half. All these events were preceded by what Wall Street likes to call "bubbles" – a delusional optimism that leads to an extreme overvaluation of assets.

The Dot Com era was famous for introducing a whole new performance metric: eyeballs, with values assigned to profitless companies based solely on web traffic. In a short time it all became entirely self-referential: the value of one dot com stock was assessed solely in relation to the value of another.

In the real estate crisis, one overly enthusiastic individual bragged in the pages of USA Today about having listed two different houses as his primary residence in mortgage applications from two different banks. This is, of course, a felony. These things seem insane after the fact, but few identified them as such at the time. So, NFTs, and, possibly, digital currencies.

A bear market in stocks usually creates a bull market in Cassandras. To echo an earlier refrain, at any given point in time there is someone predicting every possible outcome. A few of them will be right. They will loudly proclaim their rightness but keep in mind they will likely never be so right again.

Take John Paulson who became famous for shorting the mortgage market prior to the 2007 housing crash. He personally made something like $4 billion and parlayed his fame into the launch of a family of hedge funds, most of which have not come close to replicating his earlier success. One, focused on gold, lost 27% in just one month in 2013. Other Paulson funds have also struggled, leading assets to leach away, falling from a peak of about $38 billion in 2011 to around $9 billion in 2019, much of that his own money.

Of course if you're right once like Paulson was, you don't have to be right again. It's the investors who should be careful about betting on a second act. The truth is risk is difficult to assess and to measure. It's hard to know you're in a bubble until it bursts. There is always a reason stocks and other assets can go higher (or lower). Often they do. Volatility, on the other hand, can be calculated on both an absolute and a relative basis. The primary formula for this is known as standard deviation which, as it suggests, calculates variation from a mean, or average. The greater the variation, the higher the standard deviation. The higher the standard deviation, the greater the volatility.

For those of a mathematical bent, there's a further tool that can be applied to risk management, known as the Sharpe Ratio, named for William Sharpe who won the Nobel Prize in Economics in 1990. It is a second order derivative used to quantify the level of return of an asset relative to the amount of risk taken. In theory, the greater the risk the greater the return (though clearly this tends to break down at the margin when the value of an asset declines to zero).

At any rate, the Sharpe Ratio is calculated using an asset's rate of return (a stock or an ETF, for example) and the so-called "risk free" rate of return – usually some form of U.S. treasuries. The former is subtracted from the latter and the result is divided by the Standard Deviation. The higher the number, the better. In layman's terms, this suggests you're getting paid appropriately for taking a punt.

But note that like standard deviation the Sharpe Ratio also uses volatility as a proxy for risk. Like other risk proxies it doesn't really tell you whether you will make or lose money over time. It does provide some idea as to how bumpy the road to riches will be but, as a Chinese proverb may have said, you can get to the same place by many different paths. How you and your portfolio do will depend on the period measured, and on your behavior.

In general, volatility is not risk. Or more to the point, it only becomes risk when it changes behavior. The risk is, almost always, the chance that you will do something dumb. When markets go down, people will lose money but more significantly, people will lose patience. They will trade. That trading will mostly be ill-timed. The money they lose today will not compound tomorrow.

There's an interesting situation unfolding in the Peoples Republic of China. For decades, the country enforced a draconian "one child" policy. Now, China's leaders are looking around and wondering where all the people are. Not only are there fewer Chinese than there otherwise would have been, there will be even fewer Chinese in the future. The women who weren't born a generation ago are not having children now. No number of decrees can change this.

It's the same with money. Money lost today won't generate more money tomorrow. That opportunity is gone. This is what Warren Buffett has called the "permanent loss of capital," as distinct from the daily, monthly, or yearly fluctuations in the price of a stock. It is risk, as opposed to volatility. Volatility can be painful but unless it leads to self-defenestration it won't be fatal.

We were always kidding ourselves to believe that wealth inequality could forever worsen with no consequences. You don't have to look far to see the cost of all this – it's Donald Trump on right and AOC on the left. A generation enamored with Modern Monetary Theory and socialism. A worsened opioid crisis, the storming of the capitol, the trashing of Portland, Oregon. Wallstreetbets, meme stocks, and NFTs. The return of inflation. A steady sidling away from the last remnants of civility.

Academics like to refer to the uncompensated costs of environmental damage as "externalities." Anger and alienation are the externalities of wealth inequality. Those living in Latin America, in Africa know what it's like to be forever dispossessed. A few people are very rich, everyone else is very poor. The revolution ushers out one strongman and ushers in another, or sometimes the same one twice, but nothing changes.

Pushed far enough, people fight back. Sometimes they leave and head here. On balance, that's a good thing. Whether they hail from Guatemala or Herzegovina, these immigrants don't usually come to the U.S. to pursue a thousand-year-old grudge over the loss of a plot of land. They can stay home and do that. They're looking for something we once had in abundance: hope.

Kundera's Book of Laughter and Forgetting is again instructive. In cataloging the oppressiveness of life in the Soviet Bloc he describes a scene that takes place in the aftermath of the failed 1968 Prague Spring. A man is walking across Wenceslaus Square when he encounters another man throwing up. He shakes his head. "I know just what you mean," he says.

We here no longer know what he means. Pounded senseless by the never-ending chatter of the present, we've forgotten the lessons of the past, from our own experience and that of others. That most of the world has not fared well under the kind of socialism promulgated by the Soviets is true, but there's no reason to assume that democracy will always be the default alternative. History, it turns out, is neither linear nor at an end. To the extent we imagine it as a series of interconnected events it may not exist at all, as the Buddhists might say.

But it's real enough to those caught in its nightmares.

This is not just about money and it's not just about being poor. It's about how we agree to live together. One simple measure defines the problem: upward mobility. Recent data suggests this is hard and getting harder. In the U.S. just 8% of children born in the bottom 20% of income distribution move up to the top 20% as adults, well below what you find in Western Europe, a region Americans generally consider more sclerotic when it comes to creating opportunity.

Meanwhile, the top 20% of U.S. earners make about nine times more than those in the bottom. That advantage tends to compound over time. As a result, the top 5% of the population now own about 75% of the country's financial wealth while the bottom 60% has just one percent.

There's nothing good about this. It doesn't matter if you move up or not. What matters is that you believe you can. You believe that if you choose to go to school and work hard, you and/or your children can do better. You think it's not unreasonable to hope that tomorrow will be a little better than today. (Or, on the other hand, maybe hard work and sacrifice don't especially appeal to you. Maybe you'd just as soon sit this one out. But you nonetheless agree that the principle is sound. That's ok, too.)

But unfortunately, for many those beliefs are slipping away. The game seems too much weighted in favor of the house. This dissipation of hope should worry all of us, rich and poor. To put it in Sharpe Ratio terms, the excessive concentration of wealth has exposed society to a multitude of risks with little in the way of expected excess return. That's no way to run a country, or a life.

Where did everybody go?

CHAPTER THIRTEEN

Vanishing Point

A MAN. A CAR. A PLAN. Okay, not much of a plan but a guy and a car definitely – a white 1970 Dodge Challenger R/T, with a 440 cubic-inch V-8. The year was 1971 and the movie was called "Vanishing Point." Kowalski, the improbably named driver, is on a trip from Colorado to California to deliver the car to its new owner. Spoiler alert: he doesn't make it.

On one level, it's a hotrod fantasy. On another, it's redneck nihilism, a nod to French New Wave films, to Goddard, to Truffaut, to Kierkegaard. There is, as the movie implies, a point on the horizon where everything vanishes. Where it goes is unclear. For their part, investors would prefer to avoid the vanishing point. Yet evolving views of money, of currencies, and other traditional storehouses of value have the world hurtling towards it. The resolution, whatever it is, does not look especially promising.

"It takes so little, infinitely little, for a person to cross the border beyond which everything loses meaning," to again quote Milan Kundera. But what does that say to us? There's a fun BBC podcast charting the scam that was OneCoin. In it, the reporters contrast the bogus digital currency with its better known digital competitor, Bitcoin. They make the point that, unlike Bitcoin, OneCoin has no intrinsic value. The proper reaction to this is, what?

In fact, neither has intrinsic value, but Bitcoin does differ in one important way: the algorithms that create it also fix the number of coins that will ultimately be in circulation. If adhered to, this establishes scarcity. It is, presumably, better to own a scarce asset with no intrinsic value than one that both has no intrinsic value and is infinitely reproducible.

Speaking at a OneCoin "family" event, OneCoin's front woman, known as Dr. Ruja, announces that just that moment she has created a billion new OneCoins and will, effective immediately, double the number of coins each investor owns. Everyone cheers. It's unclear why. In the event, OneCoin vanished anywhere from $4 billion to $15 billion or so in real money, depending on who's counting. And Dr. Ruja disappeared, too.

So here we are. Meta currencies, which themselves have no intrinsic value, are increasingly used to purchase objects that don't exist by avatars that are, presumably, stand ins for human beings.

The charmingly bucolic FarmVille was an early iteration of this incorporeal world. The currency of the FarmVille realm, Farm Bucks, existed in a closed-loop system (i.e. they only had value within FarmVille) but the thing is, you can't always keep these meta currencies down on the farm.

So there are now what are known as "play-to-earn" games where gamers generate in-game currencies that, in some cases, can be converted back into legal tender. By one estimate, around $80 billion was spent annually on this stuff in 2021, giving rise to black markets and other trading platforms where players can upgrade farm implements or weapons and buy other equipment at a discount. Meta, the company, not the currency, has committed $10 billion to building out these new worlds, per the vision of its humanoid founder and CEO.

But like Bitcoin itself, these games and their currencies only touch the real world occasionally. As such they have value only as long as the users believe they have value. Axie Infinity is a Pokémon-like blockchain-based game that creates what its Vietnamese developer, Sky Mavis, describes as "real player-owned economies that will become places where we live, work, and play – true digital nations."

Players compete to earn in-game tokens called "Smooth Love Potion" (SLPs) using characters called "Axies." SLPs are a cryptocurrency that can be bought and sold on crypto exchanges, through this transmogrification ultimately reverting to "real" money that can buy things in the physical world.

As has been noted, the Axie revenue model looks suspiciously like a kind of Ponzi scheme – new users are required to buy into the pool through the purchase of three Axie nonfungible tokens (NFTs), costing anywhere from a few hundred to a thousand dollars. Whatever economic value can be said to exist isn't generated internally; it's a function of new players coming into the game. Should that money stop or reverse, the wheels will stop spinning.

There is, of course, a utopian argument made in support of this. In her book *New Money: How Payment Became Social Media*, Lana Swartz writes that "Many of today's dominant visions for the future of money are unlinked from the political and territorial structures of nationhood. All of these visions are, on some level, post-democracy fantasies." Sound a lot like the Axie mission statement.

But like most utopias, this one is bound to disappoint. At their heart, these are commercial enterprises. An article in the New Yorker pointed out correctly that arguments "made using utopian rhetoric – democratization, decentralization, transformation, freedom, revolution, and so on" just serve to obscure what would "otherwise be a financial conversation." It would surprise exactly no one if Facebook and its ilk turned out to be – like the British in post-Boer War South Africa – a little long on self-interest and a little short on altruism.

So Dr. Ruja is not the only one good at sleight of hand.

When money has no agreed upon social meaning, what is it worth? We talk about "intrinsic value" as if it's an idea about which we all agree. But is it? Jim Grant may value gold. Perhaps you value inner peace. Who's to say who's right? What has *intrinsic* value, value based on its own essentialness?

Jeremy Grantham is a highly successful money manager and an old school scold. He is 86 years of age, very rich, and very worried. He comes from the value school of investing in the manner of Benjamin Graham. Like all of us, Grantham sees what he sees and doesn't see what he doesn't. He sees patterns, he extrapolates trends. He may see more complex patterns and have a deeper grasp of history, but the view will still necessarily be limited.

More recently, he viewed markets as in a "Super Bubble," the result of decades of generally favorable economic, political, and demographic trends. All, or nearly all, of these are now coming to an end, he says, telling Bloomberg that "the world needs to prepare for a future of inflation, slower growth and labor shortages" as Baby Boomers age, birth rates decline, and resource extraction becomes more expensive.

He sums up his current worldview thusly: "There's only a certain amount of cheap oil, cheap nickel, cheap copper, and we are beginning to hit some of those boundaries. Climate change is coming with heavy floods, serious droughts and higher temperatures -- none of these make farming easier. So, we're going to live in a world of bottlenecks and shortages and price spikes everywhere."

Maybe. Maybe not.

In 2016, an A.I.-driven software program beat Lee Se-Dol, a top three player at the Chinese game of "Go," giving computers the title in all the major board games. (A computer defeated then-reigning world chess Gary Kasparov in 1997.) The program was developed by Google subsidiary DeepMind Technologies and called AlphaGo.

But what is interesting is not that machines are winning at chess or checkers or backgammon; that was predictable. It's *how* they're winning. They're not just taking the Ruy-Lopez opening and executing it faster or better; they're recognizing new patterns and new combinations. They're finding wholly novel ways to win. In a sense, they are, literally, playing a different game. More accurately, they don't understand what they are doing as "playing a game" at all.

Grantham has had a brilliant career but he overlooks at least one macro trend that has persisted throughout human history: a tendency towards eschatological beliefs among those in the last decades of life. If you're going to die, the rest of the world may as well end, too. But outside of our own private Metaverse other people might not necessarily see it that way. They might prefer to soldier on, in the event that something better comes along. So it's possible that when you die the world just sucks it up and opens for business the next day. Even if you're really rich.

The market crashes Grantham anticipates are of the kind generally found in textbooks. Too much credit, excess money supply, etc. There're plenty of those to go around – we may be in one now – but they're kind of unimaginative. They don't take into account the possibility that as the world moves ahead it often does so in ways not currently foreseeable and new, unexpected patterns may emerge – as with AlphaGo and Lee Se-Dol.

The mortgage crisis evaporated trillions of dollars and nearly took down the global financial system. Leverage, through mortgage-backed securities (MBS) and other derivatives, amplified the impact of thousands of ground-level speculative transactions. Matt Levine summarized the prevailing view on Wall Street at the time as "no one knew what had happened but everyone was sad."

Of course a lot of people *did* know what had happened – they were present at the creation. This included everyone from the government officials who encouraged lending to marginal borrowers to the speculators defaulting on multiple mortgages and the investment bankers slicing and dicing mortgage-backed securities into derivatives and other products whose credit ratings were increasingly removed from reality.

By the end a pervasive fin de siècle mood hung over the securities industry. Everyone knew disaster was looming. But like Prospero in Poe's The Masque of Red Death they just hoped that the tap on the shoulder would fall on someone else.

A Bitcoin crash, if and when it comes, will be highly inconvenient but the dollars involved are so far too small to imperil the real world financial system. Meta currencies in meta worlds are for the moment a triviality, but here the damage is more likely to be psychological – a further erosion in the increasingly fragile belief in the value of "real" money.

With all forms of money, look close enough and the world quickly goes quantum, whether it's Farm Bucks, Smooth Love Potions, or the Euro. Not much can stand up to a true test of inherent value. But do we really want to go out of our way to undermine belief in the dollar? As Kundera says, it's easy to cross that threshold, hard to get back.

Meta currencies and NFTs are building a fully self-referential world held up solely by faith and positive cash flow. The risk is that this faith waivers, and the world collapses, pulling belief in traditional currencies along into the ensuing abyss. If we are looking for the next really big financial disaster, it may be lurking here, in the Metasphere. But we don't want to push the financial system over this cliff. The savior for this isn't Jeremy Grantham, Allen Greenspan, or even Keynes. it's Neo from The Matrix.

Take the Red Pill.*

How do I get out of here?

CHAPTER FOURTEEN

The opposite of Meta

IN THE PREVIOUS CHAPTER WE wandered, avatar like, through the world of Meta currencies taking a wry look at their limitations. But like Bitcoin, archness is a currency with limited utility; there is still a real world out there to consider, and the arguments made concerning the metaworld do not provide a particularly useful roadmap for conducting everyday affairs in the non-meta one. If, and until, the metaworld assumes preeminence we have to live most of our lives in the one that presently exists.

Eighteen-year-old "Jala," a recent First Generation Investors graduate, is one of the individuals who populates this world. She learned about FGI while attending KIPP Collegiate, a public charter high school in Atlanta. "I didn't know what to expect," she says about her introduction to the program. "Investing wasn't something I had thought about as an option for me."

That, of course, is the problem. You don't have to spend a lifetime on Wall Street to know there might be some advantage to dropping a few dollars into an S&P 500 index fund when you're young. But you do have to know that doing this is a possibility open to you, right now, in the real world. Jala is far from alone when she says about the markets, "Before the (FGI) program I thought (investing) was just a rich people thing."

But the interest is there; it just has to be sparked. From that single Pennsylvania outpost in 2018 until today, the program has added 25 chapters around the country with 300+ volunteers seen more than 1,000 high school kids who have completed the course. And that's just the start of what co-founder Dylan Ingerman thinks is possible.

"This is going to be in every public school in America," he says.

Companies have stepped up to fund the chapters and the national organization, no doubt partly because it's the right thing to do but partly out of self interest as well. This is a world that understands self interest, and more investors and more money ultimately mean more fees. Among those providing funding in the last year or so were Goldman Sachs, TIAA, Global Endowment Management, and a unit of Northwestern Management.

In truth, the idea of investing has more of a built-in following than in the past. Meme stocks, Instagram, TikTok, and the ubiquity of the 24-hour consumer economy have created at least a baseline of awareness of the markets. Finfluencers and the ever-expanding fintech world have a vested interest in getting people involved. Behind the scenes Moore's Law has been pushing the cost of the enabling technologies lower and lower.

For most of history, if you were struggling economically your encounters with the financial world were probably not great. They mostly involved being on the wrong end of a high interest loan – for a cow, a car, a color TV, a new sofa. Even in a period of near-zero interest rates, low income borrowers have been paying up. In his review of *The Price of Time*, Edward Chancellor's book about the role played by interest rates in the economy and the world, Adam Rowe characterized the cost of money as "the rich devouring the poor."

That's true for credit cards, installment plans, and the more recent phenomenon of "buy now, pay later." It's less true for mortgages, and not true at all for equity holders. But on the debt side of the ledger, Chancellor argues that "Distributive justice requires that borrowers and lenders receive an equivalence of value." He is no doubt right, but no one lives in the world of distributive justice. In the world as it is currently configured, economically disadvantaged borrowers pay exorbitant interest rates while asset owners benefit from cheap capital. As a consequence, "... thrifty workers can't earn a decent return on their savings accounts while sophisticated speculators earn fortunes from capital borrowed for free," as Rowe says.

But so what? Historically in America the redistributionists have been loud but not very effective. This has been seen yet again in the recent Congressional debate over "carried interest," a strategy employed by a handful of people who are already rich in which income from private equity or a hedge fund is treated as a capital gain for tax purposes (and taxed at a lower rate). Though it makes no sense to do this, repeated efforts to address this legislatively have failed.

Even if the redistributionists were to be successful, their prescriptions wouldn't fix the issue of *generational* wealth inequality. What's more, there's something a little patronizing about all this. Someone is always asking someone else to do something for them, putting themselves in the position of a victim, a supplicant. A better solution would be to give everyone the opportunity to move to the other side of the ledger, to be asset owners, creating new wealth and encouraging agency.

Not surprisingly, people like this idea. Jaiylen, 17, is a student at Renaissance High School in Detroit. He was tipped to the FGI program by his mother and attended remotely from September to December 2021. The class was taught by students from UCLA.

"I wanted to further my financial literacy," he says. "Learn about stocks, bonds. Stuff that's not really taught in school."

Jaiylen put his money into a couple of mutual funds and did his research project on Zoom (the stock). "It was volatile," he says of the company, "but it was growing fast. There was a new Covid variant. It seemed like a good time to buy."

Before the class he had not been following the markets. The most important lesson learned: "diversification. A way to be a responsible investor."

FGI was launched into a bull market, but Jaiylen's class and those that followed in early 2022 ran headlong into what would prove to be a persistent decline in stock prices and the first real bout of in flation since the early 1980s. This was, in fact, the worst start to the year in 60 years, as measured by the performance of the S&P 500. But Jaiylen has mostly shrugged that off. "We're playing a long-term game," he says.

FGI is unabashedly about money. But as it turns out, money is the least of it.

"We've seen that the investing content is maybe 10-20% of the impact (on student lives)," says co-founder Cole Mattox. "The biggest thing has been the motivation of having someone two-to-three years your senior act as a mentor. They (the FGI students) get job access, exposure to universities, help applying to college."

In practice, the markets have acted as a proxy for something bigger, a knock-on effect not fully anticipated by the founders. Even at this early stage there are multiple stories of lives re-directed as a result of their participation – kids tutored by Harvard kids who ended up going to Harvard, kids who may not have bothered to graduate high school getting their diploma and heading off to college.

Why should this be? Two reasons come to mind. First, money is galvanizing, especially for those who don't have it. Everybody has heard the get-rich-quick stories – Gamestop, AMC, Wallstreetbets, "stonks." While that's not best way to learn about the markets, it's one way. In another way, sneaker trading has done something similar. It's a market, too. (Of course the "get-poor-quick" stories don't get as much play, and there are a lot more of them.)

Second, money as it is embodied in the trading of public companies opens a window on human experience. Greed, despair, etc. – it's all there on Wall Street every day. But more important to non-traders is the struggle to understand why markets do what they do. Why, for example, was the Dot Com darling Pets.com evaporated during the 2000 crash only to see its doppelganger, Chewy, seemingly doing well today? Why is Pfizer's stock up one day and down the next? Or Zoom's? Short term, who knows, but longer term there is generally something going on. You can't figure that out without research, without some understanding of how the economy works. In doing that you have to engage with the broader world in a way that forces you to acknowledge certain truths about wealth creation, and about human behavior.

Contrary to what you might read, most immigrants don't come here with the ambition of being added to the welfare rolls. They recognize that as a dead end. Toluwanimi (Toluwa" Ajani graduated from the FGI program in June 2022 and is now a student at New York University, studying business. She lives in Tampa where she attended C. Leon King, a Title One high school; the FGI program was run virtually by students from the University of Miami. Her parents came to the U.S. from Nigeria.

She learned about FGI from the Guided Pathways program, an online resource designed to help African-American students navigate the college admissions process. "I knew it was beneficial to invest," she says, but the actual mechanics were mysterious and she had no money of her own to put in the market. FGI solved for both these problems – providing an introduction to markets and financial products, and cash to put to work.

While the program encourages investing in mutual funds and ETFs, it does require that students do research on at least one individual stock. Toluwa choose Valero Energy Corp. (VLO). Her thinking: "The Ukraine crisis was going on and I thought it would be a good time to invest in an oil company."

It was a timely call: energy was one of the few stock sectors to show a positive return in 2022. But the performance is really beside the point. The value is in the discipline and analysis required for the research. She intends to keep on investing. "I see how hard my parents worked," she says. "I have to make it for my family."

The FGI curriculum took shape one week at a time, with Cole, Dylan, and Alex testing it as they went along. Says Cole, "We asked ourselves what would you need to know if you were learning investing for the first time? We didn't know what they (the students) knew and what they didn't."

"Not a lot was taught about the markets in the schools and a lot of what was taught was wrong," adds Dylan. So the three founders would meet, talk, and refine before stepping out each week to teach. Out of this came what they say is now the "preeminent curriculum for students from Title One schools to learn about the markets." But then there was another issue: how to scale.

As students with limited time they had to find a way to involve others. As a first step, they created a book, known as "the binder," that became the repository for program materials. Not just the lesson plans, but a how to manual – how to find a Title One school, how to enlist students, how to find tutors and organize a class, all the nuts and bolts of making a program work. They ultimately settled on what amounts to a franchise model: FGI provides the materials and the guidance; the colleges and universities provide the instructors and the local knowledge.

For most colleges there's a natural entry point – the investment club. You have students with an affinity for the markets and some experience investing. You have at least a few willing to commit to teaching others. Once the concept is put to them, it tends to sell itself.

"Everyone agrees this is a good idea, says Cole. "Regardless of race, creed, religion, or political disposition."

While that may be optimistic – certainly there is a dedicated Hegelian somewhere muttering darkly about this unexpected shift in the dialectic – it stands to reason that most observers would be willing to give it a try. That's been the experience on the ground. There are participating schools all around the country. They include public universities, Ivy League institutions, and historically black colleges and universities.

"Before FGI, the fact that my money can make money just never processed," says Razan Ali, who recently finished her first year at Temple University in Philadelphia. "After I finished the course, I was no longer intimidated by the idea of investing or any of that. Just money used to scare me in general. But not anymore."

That response is typical. Another example: Shelsie, who went from Boston Latin High School and the Harvard chapter of FGI to Harvard itself. "I remember this one lesson where we talked about index funds versus mutual funds. I didn't even know about index funds because all my sisters had ever done was trade and not actually invest. So I kind of felt like the stock market was a scam, like that people lose money or they get money and then lose it right after. And I was like, "I don't know how people make money out of this."

"But then I learned about index funds and how you can just put your money on the side and then hope to grow it naturally. It's been pretty cool to see that there are other sides of the stock market besides just trades."

The evidence of success is mostly anecdotal so far, but it's getting to be a lot of anecdotes. As more colleges are added and more kids go through the program the anecdotes will become data. It won't work for everyone, but it doesn't have to. A few lives redirected here and there add up.

As Dylan says, "It's about closing the wealth gap but it's more than that. Long term the question is how many students have we reached? How has it changed their view of markets? How has it changed their lives?"

The opposite of Meta.

TikTok

CHAPTER FIFTEEN

What we can conclude

THE WORLD OF INVESTING HAS undergone a dramatic transformation over the last two decades. Costs have come down. Access has gone up. At the same time, many people have become poorer, on both a relative and an absolute basis. Those are the salient facts. The question is, what do we do with them?

As our friend Matt Levine has written, the history of retail-investor-oriented investment products has not always been a good one. They are often unnecessarily complicated and too expensive. The industry itself continues to cultivate a priest-like mystique in which strategists, chartists, and others skilled in various forms of divination must intercede on behalf of the individual. Some add value; others are mostly extractive.

To paraphrase Levine: someone selling annuities with a 3-5% sales commission will definitely come to your house, bang on your door, and climb in your window to get your attention. Someone selling an S&P 500 ETF with an all-in expense ratio of 0.09% (SPY) won't. And if you only have a few thousand, or a few hundred, dollars, the annuity salesperson probably won't speak to you at all.

Some products are intended to solve short-term problems that for most people will resolve themselves over time. Volatility is a prime example. When markets go down and people get nervous low volatility funds tend to come out of the woodwork promising to help preserve capital. This protection, such as it is, comes with a cost.

These products will typically carry higher fees than plain vanilla fund, and often underperform on the upside. The entry point will be suboptimal, i.e. after the market has already gone down. Importantly, they neglect the fact that for the average investor, managing volatility is not the goal. Generating wealth over time is.

A lot of flotsam washed in on the original Internet tide – Pets.com,

Kozmo, etc. But when the tide went out the world had changed. Something similar is likely to occur with "defi," otherwise known as decentralized finance and Web 3.0. There will be a lot of roadkill, but some useful developments, too.

Interest in defi is driven by disillusionment with the traditional financial markets, and the sense among the younger generations that this world is rigged against them. This is the residual impact of the 2007-2008 Financial Crisis and the subsequent bailout. Lots of people lost lots of money then but in spite of the bankruptcy of Lehman Brothers and the collapse of Bear Stearns, they couldn't help but notice that much of Wall Street emerged from the carnage intact.

This made the idea that you could create a parallel universe that disintermediates legacy financial firms a compelling one. In practice, this world has turned out to be imperfect, too, a magnet for charlatans, with the collapse of the digital currency brokerage firm FTX in late 2022 a case in point.

For a time, FTX stood at the center of this world, having hypothecated a few billion dollars in customer assets into a $30 billion+ market cap. But then it turned out that the company was using its own imaginary token, Serum, as collateral for loans in non-arms-length transactions with its trading firm partner, Alameda, which went on to evaporate the real, dollar denominated client money. Serum seemed to derive its notional value solely from the trading of Serum (and a few other digital currencies) on the Solana blockchain. It was a classic bootstrap operation if, by tugging on your bootstraps, you could lift yourself off the floor and into the sky.

This seems to have been a common practice among token issuers. You issue the currency. You concoct a few transactions with related parties at ever increasing prices. Then you dump the coin on unsuspecting investors. Or, conversely, you mark up your portfolio to reflect the price of the last trade and then you borrow against the inflated value, an age old process familiar to the operators of bucket shops everywhere.

Chengpen Zhao, the founder of Binance and at the time a major holder of yet another FTX token, FTT, noticed all this and then dumped his holdings on the market creating an old school run on the bank. FTX collapsed in a matter of days, leaving behind a $30 billion crater in the digital currency landscape. The day before its bankruptcy filing FTX held about $900 million in liquid assets against $9 billion in liabilities, as reported by the Financial Times. Sadly, many of those assets were not so much liquid as vaporous; the tokens created and marked up by FTX. Fun.

FTX's highly fragile capital stack consisted mostly of imaginary assets, as captured in a previous era in Grant's "money of the mind." But it wasn't the only one; the initial iteration of Web 3.0 is filled with similarly fictive financing models. Some founders are no doubt attracted to this for the same reasons they would have found penny stocks scams compelling in the Web 2.0 days: the opportunity to make a quick buck.

We talked earlier about the promise of play to earn games, and there's some magical thinking going on there, too. For example: in a conversation about Axie Infinity a guest on the podcast *Hidden Forces* related that the "average player (of the game) makes around $4 a day." This, he said, was just under the average daily income of $5.50 for about half the world (World Bank data), suggesting that if we could get everyone everywhere a cell phone and a decent internet connection they could double their income by playing Axie, or some equivalent. Better living through gaming.

But these systems are inherently entropic. They require a constant infusion of new money to pay those who cash out. By now, it's clear that this kind of unravelling is a feature rather than a bug in the world of digital currencies. Earlier in 2022 a so-called stablecoin called Luna suffered a similar fate. Like FTT or Serum, Luna was conjured out of nothing and capitalized with another made-up asset. It, too, vanished very quickly.

But that's not to discount the fact that there aren't true believers. And there may be a time when there are closed-loop systems that allow people to work and play and exchange tokens in a way that creates economic value. But for now, the problem is that somewhere along the way they have to touch base with the real world. When that happens, these notional assets are repriced using real world metrics. Sometimes that price is zero.

But while the fall of FTX knocked about 25% off the going rate for Bitcoin, it did not collapse the digital currency marketplace, so possibly it will continue to exist and evolve. That, however, is the topic for another day. For now, this world is of interest to us mainly for two reasons. First, it highlights the notional aspects of all fiat currencies, including the dollar. And, second, it serves as a reminder that for most of us there's no shortcut to building wealth.

Among the economically disadvantaged there is a general unawareness as to how opportunities to invest have evolved in ways that can benefit them. Microsavings is one example. Microsavings might be thought of as the opposite of a virtual currency – pennies scraped from the daily lives of those who exist paycheck to paycheck. While it would be delusional to suggest that anyone is going to get rich this way, it would be wrong to underestimate the potential impact.

Most significantly, it can be a gateway to behavioral change. To the extent that the money saved doesn't sit idly but is put to work, it encourages some level of engagement with the world of investments, however modest. It provides a daily lesson in the operation of markets. This stands in stark contrast to the various wealth distribution schemes floated over the years. With these, individuals are just bit players.

Redistribution programs have their place but they will never be transformative. They encourage dependency. They are subject to legislative whims. Rather than continuing to try and square this circle, why not adopt something that more closely aligns the solution with economic self-interest?

Some people will look at this and say, "Yes, but money can't solve everything." These will inevitably be people who have enough money, with investment accounts at Fidelity or Goldman Sachs or Schwab, a nice car in the driveway and fully funded 529 plans for all their kids. They will sneer dismissively at the Acorns of the world and reminisce fondly about the days before no-cost stock trades and fractional shares. They will not be the people who fled Myanmar in the middle of the night. The struggles of previous generations – and their families will have had them just like everybody else – will be flicked away, ghosted.

But never mind them. The world is being moved forward by others. This includes First Generation Investors and the entrepreneur founders of various fintech firms – microsavings companies, yes, but also low cost (or no cost) trading platforms and ETFs. Some of this is wrapped in insincere blather about "democratizing" this or that but it doesn't matter. The rhetoric can be safely ignored. As always what matters in markets is whether or not it works.

All this is forcing a reconsideration of what is possible. Defi is one big idea. But just as the regulatory machine is working overtime to rein in Bitcoin and its fellow digital currencies so the traditional financial system is more likely to appropriate the best ideas coming out of Defi. Over time Defi will essentially be absorbed into the financial infrastructure.

There will, however, be benefits. For one, the mystique of the markets, used historically to befuddle individual investors and extract rents, will continue to be stripped away. Products will be increasingly accessible and costs will continue to trend down. More and more people will be drawn in, mostly for good, sometimes for not so good. But always there will be the opportunity to learn, and to improve.

For another, the accumulation phase of wealth will be switched to autopilot. That's generally a good thing. Research into the 401k marketplace has found that automatic enrollment (requiring an employee to choose to opt out of the savings program rather than to opt in) results in higher level of participation and a higher level of savings. Microsavings provides a similar opportunity, albeit on a smaller scale. You sign up and just let it run with an automatic allocation to an S&P 500 fund.

The understanding of the cumulative impact of these changes has been slow to take hold. Even as this new reality was emerging, its significance was obscured by a series of systemic crises that left many would-be investors disillusioned. It seemed sometimes that the market was determined to crush individual investors, and especially day traders and fans of "stonks." The net of this was captured in a 2021 Bloomberg story headlined, "Redditors are Right About the Unfairness of the Market." In addition to the usual market kerfuffles, the piece cited many, many curiously well-timed trades by politicians, judges, and corporate insiders. That kind of thing tends to foster a certain level of cynicism.

That's understandable, but again not helpful. While the game may be rigged in the short term, longer term it is something else, a call on growth, a wager on the future. Investing in the market is by its nature an exercise in optimism. If you think the planet is going to be hit by an asteroid next week or that global warming will soon send the ocean washing across your lawn then maybe the stock market is not for you.

But the facts as we have known them over multiple generations argue differently. Investors who measure their returns in years and decades have done fine. As our friend Grant has written, "In the long run in America the buyers have been right and the sellers have been wrong."

In sum

There's no point in rehashing the particulars of the savings crisis here. The data is easy to find and there are shelves full of books on the subject. It's depressing. It won't be solved by doing more of the same. Solving it will require more people who want to save and invest, and they will first need to have the opportunity to learn how.

The success to date of First Generation Investors provides one reason to be hopeful. The program continues to expand, adding new universities and new instructors, graduating more and more students and attracting a growing range of corporate sponsors. It's working because it's not just one more tedious iteration of how to manage credit card debt or a mortgage. Rather, it is seeking a fundamental transformation in how we view the unbanked, the uninvested. It is trying to place them in the middle of something new and powerful.

This should put paid to the idea that the economically disadvantaged are uninterested in markets. Given a chance, they are at least as interested as anyone else. It's a question of education, and of access. One often undervalued factor in helping to expand awareness – social media. There's Reddit, of course, and YouTube and Instagram. TikTok influencers are a thing, too, as The Wall Street Journal and Bloomberg, among others, have reported.

And while the advice given in these forums might be questionable, there's no doubt that they are reaching a new and different audience than the CNBCs of the world. As a Bloomberg story put it, "The rise of influencers has made talk of money less taboo."

Generation Z has found TikTok's short form videos especially compelling. In one survey, around 41% reported turning to TikTok for financial information during a one-month period, according to a story in the Wall Street Journal. As one TikToker told the paper, "A lot of people my age are living on a shoestring budget, and the advice on TikTok seems to match where younger people are in life."

Fair enough. But as always, this is a world of caveat emptor.

Service providers like Acorn, Digit, and others are also out there banging the drum. They have a vested interest in bringing people to their platforms, and they target the lower end of the market. That, too, helps to build awareness. Of late, Bitcoin and digital currency infrastructure providers have offered a few high profile lessons, some of them bad (the "have fun staying poor" meme) but others less bad (that the risk/reward relationship operates in the metaverse, too).

All of this is good; none of it is a solution unto itself. Others should be tried as well. Let a thousand flowers bloom. There will be failures as well as successes. Work will be required. But knowing this, we should not be afraid to act.

About the Author

I WAS PRESENT AT THE revolution. But this wasn't a storming of the barricades; it was the slow accretion of technological change that in the end left the financial services industry profoundly changed.

The inflection point was the introduction of the first Exchange Traded Fund, the S&P 500 Trust (SPDR, pronounced "spider") in 1993. Trading in fractional shares became widely available in 2019 when Interactive Brokers rolled out the capability across most US markets. This, combined with zero commission trades, opened up the world of stock ownership to smaller investors. Roboadvisors entered the picture in 2008, automating the asset allocation process. The first ETF to be driven by artificial intelligence was introduced in 2017 (by my firm).

I started MacMillan Communications in 1996 and we grew more or less in parallel with these industry changes. We landed our first ETF client around 2001. Twenty-plus years on we had helped introduce hundreds of new ETFs, raising billions of dollars. The idea that financial market access could be "democratized" – one we helped to advance – had clearly caught on. A thousand flowers did indeed bloom.

Of course not every person or every financial product was perfect everywhere all the time. But it was my experience that the financial services industry was overwhelmingly populated with smart, decent, industrious people. It is a profession that rewards hard work and creativity. In return, it attracts industrious, imaginative people. No surprise there. It has been a joy to be a part of it.

www.ingramcontent.com/pod-product-compliance
Ingram Content Group UK Ltd.
Pitfield, Milton Keynes, MK11 3LW, UK
UKHW060400300726

14090UKWH00001B/35

* 9 7 9 8 2 1 8 2 0 4 3 7 2 *